Who
Needs
Libraries?

challenges for
the 90s

Edited by Lewis Foreman
Librarian
Foreign & Commonwealth Office

London: HMSO
1995

STATE LIBRARIAN: Journal of the Circle of State Librarians
Editor: Lewis Foreman   **Issue No 2 1994/5**
Vol 42   no 2.

The last issue of *State Librarian* to appear in the long-familiar A4 yellow cover was Vol 39 No 3. Since then the journal has divided into two components: a monograph on a specific theme published by HMSO, and "News and Views" distributed to members by the CSL, but not available to non-members. We apologise if this has caused any confusion. *State Librarian* appears three times per year, nominally in March, July and November, though from the first issue of 1994 they will be designated as 1/1994; 2/1994; 3/1994 and not by the date as hitherto. Each year's issues, together with the relevant issues of "News and Views" will comprise one volume.

The issues published by HMSO so far under the new arrangements are:

Developing Quality in Libraries (March 1992)
   ISBN 0 11 887537 X

Developing Professionals in Information Work (July/Nov 1992)
   ISBN 0 11 887539 6

Change in Libraries and Information Services (March 1993)
   ISBN 0 11 887542 6

Performance and Potential of Librarians edited by Linda Kerr
   (July 1993) ISBN 0 11 887543 4

Market Testing and After (Nov 1993)
   ISBN 0 11 887545 0

Networking and Libraries (Nov 1994)
ISBN 0 11 887547 7

All back issues up to and including July 1993 are priced at £6.95. From Nov 1993 at £7.95. Orders should be placed with HMSO.

ISBN 0 11 887548 5   ISSN 0305–9189

Contents

Contributors

Liz MacLachlan's varied career in government libraries has included the Royal College of Defence Studies, the ODA/FCO, Central Veterinary Laboratory and the Department of Trade and Industry, where she is now Information Management Co-ordinator.

Brian Lang is the Chief Executive of the British Library. He was previously the Director of Public Affairs for the National Trust and the Secretary of the National Heritage Memorial Fund.

Andrew Lapworth is Manager of the DTI's Export Market Information Centre (EMIC) and was previously at the COI and the FCO.

Sue Hill, after a varied career as an information professional, launched a recruitment service (Instant Library Recruitment) for Instant Library. An active member of IIS Council, Sue has lectured at every library school in Britain.

Maurice Frankel, Director of the Campaign for the Freedom of Information and has been with the campaign since it was established in 1984.

John Reid has been with Silverplatter Information for nine years. John's earlier career covered business consulting, production management and civil engineering. He holds a BSc in engineering and an MSc in industrial management.

Who Needs Libraries?

Introduction: Liz MacLachlan

Department of Trade & Industry

Last year's Circle of State Librarians' conference was on market testing and after. At that time comparatively few departments had been through a market test. It was still quite new, experiences had been different, and it was hard to draw any general conclusions.

Since then, now that more departments have been through the process, what, if anything, has changed? In the early days the view was expressed that external companies were not interested in bidding for contract work. The Treasury and the Export Market Information Centre of the Department of Trade and Industry (EMIC) refuted this when they faced sharp competition from well-founded external bidders. In both cases the in-house bid team was successful. Most recently, at the end of September the Employment Department and the Health and Safety Executive in-house teams were both awarded five year contracts.

Elsewhere the review of services at the Department of the Environment—which will include a quality assessment of services provided, a user requirement and a market review—is due shortly after which the decision will be taken whether or not to proceed to a full market test. The Ministry of Defence has conducted a user survey, and a feasibility study on the future role of the library is underway. Programmes at Inland Revenue and the Lord Chancellor's Department are moving forward to different timescales.

Are we then any clearer about the way forward for government libraries after market testing? Some lessons do seem to be repeated in several departments.

The first is the difficulty in getting departments to focus clearly on what they expect or want from an information service. Defining the specification, in particular defining variations from current practice have been difficult. In some areas there is a realisation that services which should have been considered as part of the market test have been omitted, grey areas have emerged which need to be clarified, some standards have been set which are not achievable, or at least not without distortion of service elsewhere. What the department thought it wanted and what it eventually got has not been the same. There seems to be a general appreciation of the crucial importance of well focused professional and user input into the specification.

In the bidding process in-house teams have found that they must think innovatively. They must prove not only that they can meet all the mandatory and desirable requirements in the specification, but also that they can improve on them, and have a real impact on the work of their departments. Many teams have in effect redesigned their businesses in the process of preparing their bids.

Thirdly, most teams, whether defining the specification or preparing the in-house bid have found themselves hampered by a lack of real detailed knowledge of activity and costs. What are the services provided? How much time—in minutes—is actually spent on them? Who is using them? What benefit do they get from them? What are the elements of cost? How are the various overheads applied? How is the full economic cost apportioned across the services? This detailed knowledge is in my view essential to planning and managing a service at any time, but in a market testing situation the lack of such knowledge can give external competitors an important advantage.

In such a small specialism the formal mechanics of market testing, with very specific roles and the need for Chinese walls between people working at adjacent desks can prove problematic. If not sorted out early, these issues can be costly in time, distracting people from the job they have to do and causing additional stress when time is short and stress levels are already high. Where this happens it can take some time after the test result to re-establish trust and harmonious working relationships. The message seems to be to address these issues head-on at the start of the process.

Agreeing the service level agreement has also proved difficult and again professional support, both from external bodies and colleagues in government has been important. In some cases performance indicators have been applied to the service which do not accurately reflect the true nature of the work done. Performance indicators may also be very expensive in resource terms to collect. The Department of Health for example have found that they needed to invest in new IT systems to support the level of monitoring required.

In summary, although all agree that there are difficulties, market testing does seem to have led to a clarification of the relationship between the department and the library service. Even where there has been sufficient clarity in the early stages the market testing process has highlighted areas where action needs to be taken. It has also highlighted new skills required, an area which Sue Hill discusses in more detail in her paper later in this volume, and emphasised the importance of certain ways of managing in this new environment.

In this context the EMIC experience is particularly interesting as it exposes a number of issues which, although not new in themselves, have been brought together with particular force through the particular circumstances and outcomes of the EMIC market test. These are addressed in the paper by Andrew Lapworth, who is manager of EMIC and who led the successful in-house bid team, while my own paper discusses the likely impact of changes in the Civil Service on the roles we as information professionals are likely to play and the way we will need to manage.

The other papers in this volume address other challenges facing the government information profession. Maurice Frankel, Director of the Campaign for Freedom of Information assesses how Open Government legislation is being applied by departments and to what extent it has changed the culture of secrecy. John Reid, Silverplatter International, looks at the Internet, what it is and how it is being exploited, and suggests what we, as information professionals in government should be doing. In an address to the Circle AGM in November, Brian Lang, Chief Executive of the British Library, gave his vision of the future for information professionals, and we are delighted to preface these papers with his overview.

The Changing Role of Libraries

Brian Lang
Chief Executive
British Library

It is not so many years ago that libraries, and especially public libraries, were not only considered to be assets to the communities that they served but nobody would ever have thought of questioning their costs to society. The public library was taken for granted. It was considered to be a pleasant place to go to find popular reading material and information about vital issues of the day. The more specialised academic or commercial library would perform its role by supporting the advancement of knowledge in its specialist subject field. Libraries are of course still considered to be essential today and they continue to serve more or less the same purposes they have always served, but the environment in which they operate is changing rapidly. The library must justify its existence by demonstrating the demand for, and value of, its services. If the library is a part of a larger institution, it must also justify its expenditure in relation to the expenditure of the institution as a whole. And, in order to continue to meet demand, it must adjust to the frequently changing methods and techniques for handling information. In the academic sector, and to some extent the public sector too, the library must also adjust to the needs of an increasing number of students in general, and part-time and mature students in particular, to changes in teaching methods, to new performance indicators, and to new approaches to the assessment of academic institutions which put pressure on academics to undertake research and publish papers.

The recent recession and low economic growth rate have been partly responsible for the fall in library budgets. However, even without a recession, it is likely that there would have been pressure on public expenditure and libraries would have been required to manage their operations with very limited funding. Acquisitions budgets in publicly funded libraries have often taken much of the strain because they form a substantial part of "controllable" library expenditure. A common trend has been to reduce the number of journals to which the library subscribes, or avoid taking out subscriptions to new journals. However, subscription cancellations have caused publishers to increase prices to cover the intellectual worth of their titles and sometimes also to cover an increase in content. We are in a vicious circle in which higher prices prompt more cancellations which in turn prompt future price rises. Almost without exception, the prices of scientific journals have risen faster than inflation and the number of such journals has steadily increased. In Britain, the general Retail Price Index has been inflating at 2%, and the index for learned journals has been inflating by as much as 20%.

The last 40 years have witnessed the most rapid developments in the long history of communication with the advent of electronic means of representing and transmitting information of all types—number, texts, sounds, images. The electronic book is now reality. It has not emerged in isolation—it is a strand within the wider development in personal computing towards extremely small and powerful yet easy-to-use machines. Early electronic publications were mainly dictionaries and thesauri. More recent ones include bibles and encyclopaediae. Also on offer to the consumer will be video on-demand, video games, databases, educational programmes, home shopping, telephone services, telebanking, teleconferencing, and so on. The concept of the "total electronic information system" is not difficult to grasp; There are already many information services available in electronic form, ranging from bibliographic databases to financial databanks and full text databases.

However, information technology has not led to the paperless society which has been predicted. Print will not disappear. It is still as much in demand for leisure reading and some scholars need to see the originals of scholarly manuscripts for their research; surrogates would simply not suffice. But information technology has made *informal* publishing cheaper and more generally available than it would have been by conventional methods. Increasingly, authors who can contact their peer groups by sending information over networks use the networks as their main means of communicating substantial texts and, in so doing, by-pass the traditional publishing chain. However, they do not always do that because electronic publications are not yet established as legitimate and career-enhancing publications. Moreover, while the technology may have reduced the cost of informal communication, it has not necessarily made the production of formal refereed journal articles any cheaper. Indeed, the economic framework of publishing has become de-stabilised with the arrival of electronic publishing. Many publishers are reluctant to experiment with new methods of delivering publications if they cannot foresee immediate returns. Transfer from small-scale electronic journal projects to large-scale production systems requires effort and investment on a scale usually hugely underestimated. Moreover, some publishers are fearful of using technology because they are aware of the ease with which electronic data can be manipulated, changed and re-packaged into new products which may not resemble the originals at all. Such new products, if not well produced, may call into question the reputation of the publisher or may make it easy for others to market and sell new products without compensating the original copyright holders for the use of their works.

Publishers are fearful that new players can enter the market-place if they have the economic and technological power to produce impressive-looking products even if they do not have the knowledge of user needs and habits to provide the right products. Publishers' fears of a loss ownership, a lack of quality control and a loss of revenue, are, to my mind, fully justified. If electronic publishing is to succeed, the opportunities and threats of electronic publishing will need to be addressed from the producer's and the user's point of view. Indeed, researchers themselves will need to address both points of view. As authors, they provide an important source of input to the publishing system. As users, they are consumers of information. Hence, changes in the way research is published can have a double effect on them. It is likely that the impact of information technology on researchers as authors, who use keyboards to enter and edit their text, will be more significant than the impact of information technology on researchers as readers, since paper-based output will continue to be available, although the user will also have the option, in many cases, of reading from screen.

Publishers who recognise the advantages of electronic publishing may have taken to publishing in print and electronic forms, in parallel. The two versions of a text are not necessarily identical but they are usually similar enough for the user to be able to make do with one or the other. But that is not always the case. The American-based Chemical On-line Retrieval Experiment has shown that the electronic and print versions of journal titles each have advantages over one another for certain types of use. For *searching*, the electronic systems are generally easier and quicker to use than print. For *reading*, the print version is usually preferred.

So much for "IT". It is the "I" of "IT" which makes the subject meaningful. However, there is sometimes a failure to recognise that information is a resource, an input to wealth-creation, just as important as raw materials or human skills, and a key enabling tool with a commercial value to be created and maintained. It is an unusual resource in that it can be used and re-used and still exists for further use. Managers spend much of their time processing information; yet information is often mis-used. There is a tendency to generalise from specifics, to mis-represent chance fluctuations, to down-play conflicting evidence and to hear what we want to hear and ignore the rest.

Given that the amount of knowledge and information available worldwide is at present reputed to be doubling every five years, there is an urgent need to raise awareness of information itself, its availability and the value of using information correctly. It has been said that £12 million on research is wasted in the UK every day because the work has already been carried out. Simple database searches would avoid such waste. British industry suffers because of a lack of awareness of information as a resource. Information fails to flow properly; many good research ideas emanating from our universities are taken up by the Japanese and German commercial sectors, not by British companies. Surveys suggest that part of the UK competitiveness problem arises because executives do not always get the information they need. They tend to assess their performance against internal self-determined indicators and have little information on non-financial and external factors. Many companies have made large investments in information technology but there has been a tendency to adopt new computer systems without first analysing properly the purpose for which they are intended and the information required from them. If new systems simply speed up the provision of information already used by a company, then they do not heighten the company's awareness of information available from elsewhere.

It is not just private sector information which is not exploited properly. Take for example, the keel of the Australian yacht in the

1983 America's Cup race which was of a radically unusual design. The Australian entrants went to great lengths to keep the details secret. Information was withheld from the press. When the boat was lifted from the water the keel was concealed by a plastic skirt and it was said that underwater surveillance devices were used to deter divers from swimming close to the underside of the yacht. Yet, all the time the patent specification for the keel could have been inspected at several libraries in the UK.

Earlier discussion about company investment in information technology brings me on to the importance of not taking decisions solely on the basis of the availability of the technology. There is always a temptation to do something simply because it has become technically possible, but there are plenty of commercial failures from that approach. Innovations in services or products should always develop from a clear market demand of latent need, and the market should be identified before taking up novel technological opportunities, and particularly so in the case of electronic publishing which requires substantial capital investment at the outset.

Most publicly-funded libraries in the UK are, or recently have been, subject to heavy review. The British Library produced a statement of strategic objectives last year and from those objectives identified four priority themes which are driving forward its plane. More recently, the "Follett" review of higher education sector library services has led to a number of well defined activities in information technology and has given impetus to special collection development and the development of a framework for a national strategy for library provision for researchers. Public libraries are currently under review. The future shape of their services is being mapped out and the possibility of contracting out certain services is also being investigated. Moreover, representatives of public libraries, academic libraries and the British Library have recently put forward recommendations for building on existing good relationships among the players in their respective sectors, under the aegis of the now defunct Library and Information Services Council for England. Those recommendations are intended to build upon such initiatives as the Library and Information Plans which have helped to co-ordinate library and information services in many parts of the UK. Many types of information provider have been involved from the public and private sectors. The purpose has been to provide a framework within which planned co-operation and co-ordination of services could take place, making best use of the resources available.

Despite these initiatives, the role of libraries is not assisted by the current fragmentation of responsibility of information-related activities among government departments. The DTI looks after information technology, the regulation of intellectual property and other matters; the Cabinet Office looks after the Office of Public Service and Science and, through CCTA, promotes the efficient use of information and information technology in government departments; the DNH supports the British Library and oversees public libraries; the Department of the Environment supports public libraries; the Department for Education is responsible for policy on school, college and university libraries and so on. I am pleased the Secretary of State has recently announced that a new co-ordinating body will be set up in January 1995 to provide the government with a single, authoritative source of advice on library and information issues. However, I am disappointed that Scotland and Wales will not be fully represented by the new Library and Information Commission. It remains to be seen how successful the new body will be in co-ordinating library and information policy and practice across the UK.

How are libraries reacting to the changes taking place around them? Many libraries are already able to use electronic networks to send and receive information. This practice is becoming widespread and is changing the unit of library development from the national or regional level to the international level. National boundaries are becoming irrelevant as libraries begin to rely on electronic databases held in other countries. But we must not become too reliant upon other countries just in case political changes overseas restrict use of their databases. In the UK, the higher education sector has for a number of years been using the Joint Academic Network to exchange information. Some industrial and commercial companies have their own company-wide electronic networks which are used for transmitting company documents around the world. Partly for security reasons, those companies do not yet make use of a single electronic network. The current review of public libraries recommends that they should be connected to a nation-wide network. The likelihood is that, once issues of security and charging have been resolved, all libraries in the UK will have access to the same nationwide electronic network. That does not mean that they will all use the facility, but the facility will at least be available.

What will they use the network for? They will use the network for sharing bibliographic and catalogue records, for informal communication and, increasingly, for the transmission of journal articles. The advent of electronic networks and the availability of electronic publications presents new opportunities for libraries to change their collecting policies. An electronic library need not be held under one library roof or any other single roof. It may be distributed among many sites belonging to different institutions. There is less need than there was for libraries to hold comprehensive collections just in case they are required. Libraries will be able to obtain electronic texts from elsewhere. They will be able to extend their activities beyond their main collecting functions to become information, education and leisure centres. One of the current trends is towards the principle of "just in time" document supply.

However, changes will not necessarily come about as quickly as the technology will allow. Libraries, traditionally, have been reluctant to change. Once a library starts subscribing to a journal, natural inertia and the desire not to break a run are strong forces towards continuing the subscription unless financial pressures force them to do so. Moreover, libraries which consider themselves to be strong in certain subjects may be reluctant to rely on other libraries' holdings in those subject areas even if they are made available to them over networks. Then there are the conditions and methods of access to be sorted out. The Copyright Act of 1988 which provides a framework for the copying of printed publications does not apply to electronic publications. There are no formal and generally accepted methods of access or conditions of use for them. It seems likely that, at least in the short term, libraries wishing to acquire electronic texts from publishers will need to make arrangements with each publisher about conditions of use and royalty payments. There could be one royalty rate for viewing a document and one for printing.; one for remote access and one for local access; that is, provided all those types of access are permitted. What will be an appropriate level of charge? And who should pay—the library or the user?

The conditions and types of use arrived at are likely to influence the technical solution chosen to store and archive electronic publications. Will it be a system which allows national or international access to any of the institutions which have signed up to a particular network? Or will it be a system which only allows access to users who visit the premises? In this latter case, would there be a central point of access in the library or would access be permitted at terminals on every desk? There are many technical possibilities for storing and archiving electronic publications. Information technology planning and implementation will become a major cost component of library expenditure. Will it lead to any savings? Or, will cost reductions have to be made? Could revenue be made and, if so, how should this be done?

The availability of electronic documents does not only raise the question of what should be purchased for the Library's collection and what should be obtained from elsewhere, in response to demand. It also raises the questions for those libraries which do acquire the electronic products, of maintenance and preservation and of bibliographic control. How will bibliographic control be ensured? There are major implications for the creators of bibliographies and catalogues. The continued growth of printed publications in itself creates challenges in currency and coverage, added to which are the challenges of adapting record formats if necessary to cater for non-print publications.

There is much debate about preservation and the form it should take. It is clear that the scale of the problem is huge and far exceeds the resources available in most libraries. Apart from the resource issues, there is also the need to decide when it is sufficient to preserve the intellectual content and when the physical form should be preserved. Some of the newer publishing media offer a reasonable medium-term option which could save millions of existing volumes on acid paper. The archival properties, durability, hardware and software obsolescence all need to be taken into account in determining appropriate preservation publishing media.

It is likely that libraries will become gatekeepers and facilitators for electronic information resource provision. The Library could provide access either through computer-produced prints from the supplier or through on-line systems, for reading at the screen or printing out at the terminal; another option would be for the library to obtain permission to download material from databases on agreed terms and exploit the material for the benefit of its users. Or, the library could acquire copies of electronic databases for use in the library. But should libraries be used at all? They could be bypassed and information supplied directly to the user who would pay for use according to a specified formula. While many questions remain about the future role of the library, my prediction is that libraries will help publishers to match their products to users' requirements. Librarians do not wish to go out of existence. They wish to have a role. And they *will* have a role because they understand what the reader requires and how to deliver services. However, library staff will need to train themselves and their users in the methods of gaining access to information held in electronic form. It should not be underestimated how long the period of transition from traditional to new library services may take. The support infrastructure which comes into play today when things go wrong should be replicated in the world of electronic access.

You will probably wonder what the British Library is doing about all these developments. Although the British Library is a young Library, formed in 1973, it has brought together a great number of collections some of which date back 250 years. The richness and variety of the collections can be seen from some of the Mughal manuscripts, to the world's earliest dated printed book, the Diamond Sutre, from Chinese oracle bones of the second millenium BC, to the latest medieval texts. Many countries cannot chronicle adequately their histories without recourse to the British Library. Our archive is gradually being extended to include non-print materials. We have several million reels of microfilm and microfiche, many of which contain long runs of research collections. We have also one million sound discs and over one thousand CD-ROMs containing the images of one million patents. We also have 400 biomedical journal titles on CD-ROM. Our electronic texts include items from our collections which we have digitised so that we can preserve the originals and make the information available, over networks. We have just digitised the thousand-year-old manuscript of Beowulf and made test images available over the Internet.

The British Library is a massive archive. But our aim is to be much more than an archive. We must catalogue our collections, promote them, make them widely available and offer information services based on them. And we must continue to develop our collections and provide access to other libraries' specialist collections if we are to continue to perform the functions expected of a national library.

The variety of our collections is such that no single catalogue could satisfy all our users' requirements. The Library produces both general and specialist catalogues. The largest catalogue is the General Catalogue of Printed Books which contains four million records of books published all over the world, in all languages and scripts from the beginning of printing to the 1970s. The Library also produces the *British National Bibliography*, containing well over one million records and covering the whole output of British publishing since 1950. The Library has its own database host system, BLAISE-LINE, containing over thirteen million records. We are heavily involved in producing CD-ROMs of catalogue data and many of the records available on-line are also available on CD-ROM.

We are moving towards making our collections readily accessible around the world. We aim to do this by letting users know what is held, making it easy for them to identify and ask for documents, and by delivering a significant proportion of the holdings electronically within minutes. The current carrier is the fax machine which enables the Library to transmit the contents of a printed work to any destination which has a fax machine. However, we have begun to seek permission from publishers to transmit their electronic texts or electronic versions of their printed texts over networks.

The British Library seeks more effective use of its existing resources by co-operating and collaborating with the library and information community at home and abroad. Libraries in the UK are generally keen to cooperate with one another. Efficient co-operation can provide users with much higher levels of service by giving access to other libraries' collections through inter-library lending. Duplications in collecting may be kept to a minimum. Generally, it is recognised that sharing resources leads to considerable savings. The Library is heavily committed to post "Follett" work and has begun to investigate how it can meet the changing needs of its academic users by undertaking a study to assess the feasibility of a British Library "universities research support service". We hope to be able to establish a similar relationship with public libraries when the current review has been completed. And our membership of CBI draws us closer to the needs of our industrial users.

The legal deposit system in this country—which includes the national libraries of Scotland and Wales, and the university libraries of Oxford, Cambridge and Trinity College, Dublin, besides the British Library—has been of inestimable benefit. Over the past year, the British Library alone received about 370 thousand items through legal deposit. Attempts are being made to ensure the whole legal deposit system operates efficiently among the six legal deposit libraries. Agreed collecting policies are being explored, so that not all of the six libraries need to have complete sets of legal deposit material. A shared cataloguing system is also in place so that record creation is kept to a minimum. Considerable financial savings will be achieved through this kind of co-operation.

But the existing legal deposit system has a drawback in that it applies only to print. Because it does not take in new electronic media, microfiche and other non-print publications, our collection of national output is therefore incomplete. If we are to fulfil our responsibility to care for the national published archive, then statutory deposit needs to cover new media as well as print on paper. The British Library has begun to consider what will be required in a proposal to Government for the legal deposit of non-print. The proposal may well be a joint one from the Library and other organisations which house parts of the national published archive. Three major strands in the proposal to government will need to be developed. The first is why we think non-print needs to be the subject of statutory deposit. The second aspect is to investigate exactly what will be collected, and how. The third aspect is to assess the resource requirements for the handling of non-print. What resources will be needed to record, catalogue, shelve, store, preserve and provide access to non-print publications?

On the overseas front, the Library is working with the Library of Congress on the creation of a single authoritative list of the authors of more than 100 million works held by the two libraries and on a review of the principles for harmonising the US and UK MARC formats in an effort to increase compatibility between them. In Europe, the Library is heavily involved in an EC programme of research to improve European bibliographic resources. It is also a member of the Consortium of European Research Libraries which has begun to establish a database of all European printing of the hand-press period. We have recently strengthened our relationships with the British Council which provides an agency service for us in many parts of the world and assists in the arrangements of British Library conferences and exhibitions as the need arises.

At home, the Library longs for the day when it will be able to occupy its new premises at St Pancras. The environmental conditions for the storage of books will be much improved; the London-based reference collections will be integrated for the first time; and the new opportunities being made available by technological development will be capable of being grasped in the new building. A particular feature of the new building will be the extensive provision of automated services which are being designed specifically for St Pancras. Our new building will provide us with an identity of our own. The current construction problems, which are not of the Library's making will fade into insignificance. The building will be a shell. It will be an important shell that will contain the thoughts and aspirations of human beings and will preserve for posterity our past.

A presentation of this kind can reach no conclusions. My aim has been to raise a few points which can easily be overlooked in the world of information technology. Suffice it to say, the future for of libraries and library services should be driven by user needs. The approach taken should be as simple as possible; users will always be drawn to services which give readily usable information. The implementation of information technology in itself is not impeding developments. It will become more pervasive as solutions are found to some of the economic, marketing, social and legal issues. The key to successful electronic library systems will be co-operation among librarians, publishers and users. I have no doubt that libraries will have traditional and electronic components in active co-existence with one

another. To that extent, the notion of the library has changed funda-
mentally whether we wish this to happen or not.

References
1. Follett, Sir Brian: *Joint Funding Councils Libraries Review Group:
    report*. Higher Education Funding Councils for England, Scotland
    and Wales, 1993.

DAWSON ON-LINE SERVICES

BOOKS

Government Libraries After Market Testing: the way forward

Liz MacLachlan

Information Mangement Co-ordinator, Department of Trade and Industry

One of the important indicators of the way the future is likely to shape up is the White Paper on the future of the Civil Service. *The Civil Service: continuity and change*[1], was presented to Parliament by the Prime Minister, the Chancellor of the Exchequer and the Chancellor of the Duchy of Lancaster in July. As its title suggests the white paper looks both backward, to sum up what has been achieved so far, and forward to determine our future direction.

At the outset the white paper confirms the basic principles on which the Civil Service is based:

- **ministerial responsibility** with ministers accountable to Parliament for what is done in their departments and agencies;

- **basic principles** the key role of integrity, political impartiality, objectivity, selection and promotion on merit;

- **core standards** a minimum framework of rules and standards of behaviour set centrally, to be reflected in local regulations.

It goes on to place itself firmly within the context of the changes to the way that the Civil Service is managed since the Fulton report of 1968—the Financial Management Initiative, Next Steps, the Citizen's Charter (including the Competing for Quality initiative which launched market testing) and finally Open Government.

It then sets out what it calls "levers for change"—the tools which have been effective in the past, and which will be extended in the future. They are:

- **continued emphasis on outputs and performance targets** as measures of efficiency;

- **tight control on running costs**. Each department will draw up annual efficiency plans to deliver savings which will be monitored but not directed by the Centre. Control through manpower targets is explicitly rejected, although the government "would expect Civil Service manpower to fall significantly below 500,000 over the next four years."[2]

- **better management information systems** to support the efficiency plans, and a move to resource accounting systems which are closer to those used by the private sector;

- **more delegation to departments and agencies** to decide for themselves
    - how they achieve their efficiency targets. In essence they will be able to decide to market test, privatise or contract-out without having centrally set targets
    - their pay and grading levels
    - their management structures. The White Paper gives a clear steer to de-layering, removing certain grades altogether to give more direct reporting lines

- **encouragement to departments to use management techniques** such as benchmarking and process re-engineering to re-examine what they do, how they do it and what they can learn from others about ways to do it better;

and finally

- **emphasis on the need to train and develop staff** to support the greater responsibility they are expected to bear. Specific mention is made of Management Development Programmes, National Vocational Qualifications and the Investors In People award.

Proposals for the Senior Civil Service are particularly interesting. These are based on the Efficiency Unit report *Career Management and Sucesssion Planning*, the Oughton report published last year[3], with some additional proposals. They propose:

- **the creation of a new Senior Civil Service** for the range of responsibilities currently at Grade 5 and above;

- **open competition** to be considered for posts at this level. Advertising posts is strongly encouraged where a strong field is required, or new blood sought;

- **more exchange with the private sector**, and more interchange between departments and with agencies;

- **written contracts of employment**, fixed term and rolling as appropriate;

- **flexible pay**, performance related, with more pay variation based on wider pay ranges.

Although still only a white paper, *Continuity and Change* is a very important document for the future shape of the Civil Service. Its major thrusts are for greater delegation to departments to create the management structures they need to run their businesses and a move towards the techniques and conditions in the private sector. Departments are considering now how to implement these proposals, and the first effects will start to be seen from next year, although it will be April 1996 before the major changes are implemented.

At the same time government is in the middle of a fundamental review of departmental spending. Each department has been asked to examine the long term trends in its spending on individual programmes to assess whether they are sustainable. The aim is to find areas where the State might withdraw altogether, or where better targeting is appropriate. The first reviews fed into last year's Budget, and we can expect to see more from the next batch, which includes the Treasury itself, in this year's budget on November 29. This will lead to major changes in the work that departments do, and consequently to the staff they need to do it.

Taken together the white paper and the Fundamental Review programme amount to very considerable change to the purpose and shape of the Civil Service. What will it mean for libraries?

Our customer base will change. Market testing has already meant that some areas that used to use our information services such as IT, internal consultancy or training provision, have gone to external contractors with their own arrangements. Major changes to the business of the department will mean changes in the stock we buy, the services we provide and the expertise required to run them. Smaller, leaner departments will lead to smaller, leaner information centres. Policy makers have traditionally been those who have been the hardest to convince of the value of external information. If they come to predominate in the departments of the future, what can we offer them?

There is a recognition in the white paper of the importance of information, in particular management information, to support managers. The Efficiency Unit is conducting a scrutiny of departmental systems, aiming to identify lessons and best practice. As information professionals, we have a great deal of expertise in handling information from a huge variety of sources, both internal and external, and in structuring it so that it makes sense. The door is, if not half-open, at least ajar. Increasingly, with the highly publicised failure of computer systems such as London Ambulance, there is a recognition of the "I" part of "IT". Several departments have already recognised their need for information management and formulated information policies. Others are considering doing the same. We need to push hard to make sure that our knowledge of how people use information and our expertise is drawn on by departments in designing their systems.

We will also need to change *our* management structures. It is results that matter, and we will need to be flexible so that we can change as our customers change. Staff must really know what customers want, and have the right skills to deliver it. We must change our focus from stock and services, to spotting changing demands, new opportunities and to developing the products to satisfy it. We must make sure that our purpose is clear, so that staff know where we are going and what is expected of them. We need to develop flatter, less hierarchical structures, to speed up communication, so that the people who know what the demands are have the authority to deliver them and so that changing trends are spotted fast. Business planning techniques, project management and training strategies are crucial.

Change is not only internal. Changes in technology are making computer systems more user friendly. The skills base is increasing, more and more people use word processors, Spreadsheet and databases as naturally as they use pen and paper. Office systems and networks are becoming much more pervasive, and the increased accessibility of information sources such as external databases and CD-ROMs are leading to a greater demand for end-user searching. This can be viewed as a threat, customers satisfying their information needs without access to the library. But the experience in government suggests that it is much more of a challenge and an opportunity.

Networks give the library the opportunity to raise awareness of information, and co-incidentally of the library itself. On the day of the last Cabinet reshuffle the Department for Education Information Bureau and Library (IBL) was putting details of the new ministerial appointments onto the electronic bulletin board for the entire department as the news was announced on the television. They then extracted biographical details of the main appointments from a database held in the IBL, and posted it onto major noticeboards, including the one outside the canteen, by lunchtime. The library of the Defence Research Agency at Malvern networks CD-ROMs around the site, and is looked to as experts not only for the information, but also for this sort of technology. The same is true of the Department of Health amongst others.

The role of information professionals in government is changing and changing fast. We are moving away from being mainly the providers of raw information, and the new opportunities are, I believe, very exciting. So what are they?

I have been writing forward plans and mission statements—and even vision statements—for nearly ten years. In that time the words may have changed, but the basic idea has not. The role of the information centre is still to make sure the right information gets to the right people at the right time in a form they can use immediately.

As our customers become more expert in using electronic networks it will be our job to make sure that they find the right information. We will need to evaluate the quality of information available. As information professionals we know how the database providers collect their information and how often they update it. We know that some sources are better than others at answering particular sorts of questions. The natural place to look for company accounts is ICC, but if you only want the chairman's statement, or the section headed "pensions" it would be better to use MAID because sections can be downloaded individually. The exchange rate will determine whether it is cheaper to download information from Datastar in Berne or Dialog in the US. It will be our role to pass this on to our customers so that they can make informed choices of sources and be able to evaluate the answers they get back. The old saw about librarians—I don't know the answer but I know where to find it—will be just as true in the future as it has been in the past. The Internet will be hugely important as an information channel and source in the future. Facilitating and guiding end-users could be our job, if we grab it.

It will also be our job to be facilitators, to help users with the business of getting online. There are a number of products already, either independent such as Communicator, or developments of an online host such as Infoplus from FT Profile, which sit between the searcher and the user and help them prepare a search, get connected, use Boolean and keep a check on costs. These are of limited use to us, because we know what we are doing, but are designed for non-expert end-users. Finding, evaluating and promoting these products for our customers will be important. Training is also important. We can either provide direct training or facilitate, evaluating courses and advising on the right external training for individual users.

We have a marketing role for information. It will be up to us to keep close to the market and evaluate new products as they come out. We are setting outselves up to be experts in information so we must make sure that our knowledge is fully up-to-date. We need to keep close to our organisations so that we know about and can anticipate its changing needs. We will also draw closer to the information providers, negotiating with them on terms and licences, but also in developing their products to suit what our customers need and want.

A distinguing quality of information, which bedevils attempts at cost-benefit analysis, is that it has no value except in use. We need to organise information so that it is usable directly by individuals. This can mean a lot of things, from putting hot topics up on a bulletin board to downloading financial information into a spreadsheet to doing detailed research and interpreting the meaning of the information we find. In his book on the learning organisation Peter Senge[4] talks about managers becoming designers or architects, concentrating on the structure within which people work rather than day-to-day operations. We must become the architects of the information systems in our organisations, providing some information directly and signposting to other sources, such as CDs or external databases or the experts in the library as appropriate. We need to design the tools—indexes, abstracts, thesauri—to help users navigate around these systems. Knowledge comes from linking information. We will be less and less concerned with building databases and collections, more and more with linking disparate pieces of information from a variety of sources, then remembering where we found them.

So the future roles of information professionals will combine knowledge of sources and the techniques of finding, organising, and storing information with those of designer, consultant and counsellor. Marydee Ojala has written about possible future titles for librarians to reflect their changing functions[5]. But whether you decide to be a Cybrarian or a Director of Knowledge Management, an Information Czar or a Corporate Intelligence Professional the basic job of getting the right information to the right person at the right time will still be there. Our users will still need "libraries". Whether it is from us or from somebody else is up to you.

References

1. *The Civil Service: continuity and change.* Cm 2627 HMSO, 1994.
2. *op cit* p 30.
3. Cabinet Office, Office of Public Service and Science, Efficiency Unit. *Career Management and Succession Planning Study.* (Oughton report). HMSO, 1993.
4. Senge, Peter M: *The Fifth Discipline: the art and practice of the learning organisation.* Century Business Books, 1993
5. Ojala, Marydee: "What will they call us in the future?". Special Libraries 84(4), Fall 1993, pp 226–234.

Partnerships & Market Planning: a case study of the DTI's Export Market Information Centre (EMIC)

Andrew Lapworth

Manager, Export Market Information Centre

> *"In the business jungle there is a clearing. The natives call it the market place".*[1]

The Department of Trade and Industry's Export Market Information Centre (EMIC) is not a typical government library. The overwhelming majority of its customers are members of the public: business people, market researchers, consultants and other business and export researchers. The centre is best seen as a business library provided by the export promotion divisions of the department for the benefit of UK businesses researching overseas markets. Nevertheless, because of EMIC's unique collection of overseas data and mix of information on export markets it represents a key internal information source, complementing the other library services within DTI.

However, EMIC is still a government library; since its inception as the Statistics & Market Intelligence Library (SMIL) it has been run by government librarians and has traditionally enjoyed close professional links with the main DTI Information & Library Services (ILS); for example, librarian grades move between ILS and EMIC posts in the normal course of their development. We are perhaps examples of librarians "outbedded" (to coin a Rayner scrutiny phrase) to the Overseas Trade divisions.

The 1993–1994 EMIC Market Test demonstrated many of the classic or model features of the market testing process. However in the EMIC case one new process or management tool was introduced: *Market Planning*, and a new option, or route known as "*Partnerships*" (otherwise known as *partnering arrangements*). Both of these two features have subsequently been incorporated into the resulting Service Level Agreement (SLA). This paper will examine these novel features as potential indicators of one way forward for government libraries "after market testing".

To set the context, in 1993 the prior options for EMIC were:

- abolish it, as an unnecessary function of DTI;
- privatise it, if it had demonstrable value;
- contract it out directly;
- or, market test it.

The model features of the EMIC Market Test process were:

- the service to be market tested could be clearly defined;
- a Market Test Steering Group was set-up;
- a full customer survey was commissioned to gauge demand for the service and to confirm it was worth market testing (customer surveys showed it was!);
- staff were in place (and keen) to mount an In-House bid;
- the client-side/In-House split was established;
- the User Requirement was defined and described;
- an advert alerted bidders to the market test;
- pre-selection followed from 12 expressions of interest;
- organisations were sent a detailed Statements of Requirements (SOR) and an Invitation to Tender (ITT).

From my In-House perspective, we:

- set-up an In-House team;
- completed a thorough review of our service;
- obtained, through open competition, our own management consultants to assist us:

- to do detailed costing of the existing service using internal DTI guidance on Market Test costings;
- to do another review of our service from their own, external, perspective;
- to help us examine critically the ITT and SOR, line-by-line, mandatory requirement by mandatory requirement to ensure full compliance;
- to review and review again HOW we could both comply with the SOR, and make economies, and demonstrate innovation and increased value for money (VFM);
- to sell the benefits of our bid more positively;
- to edit our tender document.

To cut a very long story short, of the six organisations invited to bid only three responded; the In-House team and two external competitors. On the 16 March 1994 the Market Test was awarded to the EMIC In-House team.

Market Planning

Market Planning is a concept well established in the commercial world. In EMIC we found it helpful in both, submitting our original bid, and subsequently in delivering services on behalf of our department. There is evidence of this process being increasingly applied to libraries.[2][3]

The Marketing Plan is now at the heart of the EMIC service. The In-House tender already contained a draft Business Plan, but the Marketing Plan ensures services are focused on the market, and the benefits derived by customers.

Market Planning has been defined as "the systematic application of marketing resources to achieve marketing objectives".[1] It is designed to infuse the whole of EMIC's structure and ensure managers and units of different functions work together rather than pursue their own functional objectives in isolation. In our case it shows clearly how all our efforts (including initiatives and actions already described in our tender) are based on meeting objectives relevant to the specific user needs of different segments of our markets (ie different types of customers or users). Adopting a Marketing Plan has helped ensure we keep the focus of our service on the varying wants and needs of our customers. Our managers' efforts are more closely based on matching our resources to customer needs.

In taking a Marketing Planning approach we looked at EMIC, its information resources and services, in terms of the four "Ps" of Marketing:

- Products: the information sources acquired and made available, and the service offered to customers;

- the Price; EMIC, as a self service research facility is currently a service without admission or usage charges; however, the *price* for customers needs to be appreciated; customers will price for themselves the cost of using a "free" service. On a more specific level we monitor the costs of the services we offer, such as photocopying, online and CD-ROM searching, and the level of charges for the publications we sell;

- the Promotion of the service: who are we targeting? How do we reach target markets (eg Small & Medium sized enterprises)? What is our message to each target group of customers? Where and how should the promotion be delivered?

- the Place: where it is made available.

To undertake a Marketing approach and produce a plan the process therefore included:

- a marketing audit of our four Ps;

- a SWOT analysis (Strengths & Weaknesses of EMIC as viewed by customers and the Opportunities open to EMIC and the external Threats facing it);

- our planning assumptions;

- setting our objectives and strategies;

- development of detailed programmes of action (for individual managers and their sections).

Marketing Planning is a *process*. The Plan itself is designed to be a working document which will be kept under review at regular marketing meetings. For example, the first Plan includes programmes for a twelve month period.

The In-House bid tender contained a detailed Training Programme for EMIC staff, which sets out training objectives and the ways in which they will be achieved, using a mixture of internal and external training events: induction and on-the-job training, external courses, computer assisted learning, professional reading etc. Marketing and Marketing Planning is not something that comes naturally to all librarians. Therefore the Marketing Plan includes a Training Programme for key

EMIC Managers in the market planning processes, and emphasises training in promotional activities as essential for most EMIC staff.

Those interested in Marketing planning, should see Sheila Webber's feature on marketing in *Inform*, a useful overview which includes a survey of recent books and articles on marketing information services[4]. On the Marketing Planning process itself I would additionally recommend *The Marketing Plan: a pictorial guide for managers*, by Malcolm McDonald and Peter Morris[1].

The Partnering Route

As indicated earlier, there were four prior options open to the Department in looking at EMIC; these arose out of the policy framework set out in the 1991 white paper, *Competing for Quality; buying better public services*[5]. At the tail end of the EMIC Market Test a new option, or route arose: *Partnering*.

Partnerships is now a common buzz word. Wherever you look companies are setting up partnerships with their major suppliers. According to a recent survey by the Partnership Sourcing Group[6] nearly 75% of purchasers and 61% of suppliers use Partnership sourcing. What does it mean? One definition is:

> "a system in which purchasers and suppliers seek to set-up long term, collaborative relationships with each other based on more than cost analysis."[6]

In industry, companies are becoming more aware that creating value depends on the links between their suppliers and distributors. The jargon is "vertical co-ordination"; companies cannot only be content with their own performance, but must also be willing to improve the performance of their distributors and their suppliers. There are an increasing number of examples of public-private sector partnerships infusing government initiatives and services.

In our case, in making their decisions, DTI Ministers asked for interesting features offered by the two unsuccessful bidders to be explored where new or innovative services to customers would result.

For EMIC this has meant inviting our two direct competitors in the Market Test (the British Library's Science, Reference and Information Service (SRIS) and a joint venture (JV) by the Institute of Export and Business & Trade Statistics Ltd) to work in a partnering arrangement with us in providing additional new services for customers. With The British Library EMIC is working more closely with the Business Information Service in SRIS on better signposting to each other's services. There is closer staff liaison through short term job swaps, and participation in each other's in-house training, and the EMIC and BIS are jointly working to provide a new service making available the older statistical material unique to EMIC via the British Library's Document Supply Centre at Boston Spa; the latter will improve customer access to longer runs of the some of the unique overseas national statistical series obtained by EMIC. In the longer term we are exploring the viability of mounting the EMIC online catalogue on a British Library database.

With The Institute of Export led Joint Venture we are working on the provision within EMIC of new sources of trade statistics on CD-ROM and a new fee-based research service based within EMIC (using EMIC's and the JV's combined resources). The latter service is a significant step for EMIC. The new research service will involve JV sponsored information staff working in EMIC, alongside existing EMIC staff, serving different segments of the same broad customer base.

Why go the partnering route? For the Department a partnering arrangement may be more appropriate than market testing where:

- there is no reason to retain all the service delivery in-house;
- the market is not developed;
- functions, or technology are changing rapidly;
- there are higher risks in direct contracting-out.

A partnering arrangement can:

- enable a service to get closer to core activities;
- combine public and private sector stengths;
- allow a planned transfer of activities and functions;
- provide flexibilities in developing the service for the benefit of customers;
- provide more managerial control of change.

What are the benefits? Our partnering arrangements are still being formed so these are initial views and expectations. Firstly—and most importantly— this has enabled EMIC to serve a segment of the market not hitherto served: customers who want to pay for data extractions to be done for them and despatched to them. The exact level of market demand for such a service is unknown; risk is shared by EMIC and its partners. Secondly, without any increase in EMIC staff resources the Centre has introduced a new service. Thirdly, EMIC will have gained the benefits of working in a partnering arrangement with the IoE with it large membership and customer base; from the IoE's partner Business & Trade Statistics Ltd, EMIC has gained access to new statistical sources and the company's expertise and network of contacts within trade statistics, one of EMIC's core data sources. Fourthly, with the British Library, EMIC is improving the marketing of our respective services to a common segment of the customer base. Lastly, EMIC and BL staff will benefit from more formalised networking and sharing of information and training.

The advantages of the partnering arrangement have also come in parallel with the benefits obtained from the market test process itself. EMIC now has more and better information about who uses its services and why; staff and customers have a clearer perception of the role of the service. For the EMIC team the SLA is explicit about both the sort of service the department wants and the services to be provided to customers. In the EMIC case the SLA is drawn up between the Export Data Branch (EDB) representing the DTI, and the In-House team as the chosen service supplier. EDB has taken over from EMIC the responsibity for measuring customers' satisfaction with EMIC and will in future report the findings to the EMIC team at regular EMIC Management Board meetings.

The SLA also contains quantitiative performance measures (eg hours the service is provided, number of customers to be handled etc). These will be promulgated to ensure customers know the criteria for judging the performance of the service and how far EMIC is meeting them.

Therefore, following the EMIC Market Test and adopting a partnering arrangement and following a Marketing Plan, it may be useful here to summarise what has changed and what is still the same. Firstly, what is still the same:

- The basic service provided by an In-House team;
- the continued collection of management information;
- consulting & listening to customers;
- similar core EMIC management structure;
- EMIC still subject to departmental planning and budgeting processes.

We may construct a somewhat longer list of the innovations:

- The SLA makes requirements more explicit;
- a slimmed-down staff structure, but with additional professional posts;
- a marketing-led approach, with greater focus on the Marketing Plan;

- new services to be provided in partnering arrangement with external bodies;

- enhanced collection of management information, with shift of responsibility from service deliverer to client side (who have new responsibility for collecting management information and measuring customer satisfaction);

- a new EMIC Management Board set up by the client side, now including representatives from key customer segments;

- clearer financial reporting lines and new budgetary delegations, including for the first time for marketing and direct promotional activities;

- in itself the Market test has raised the profile of EMIC both within the department and with customers and potential customers;

- a specific outcome has been the acknowledgement of the need to promote EMIC better to its target customers; this now features as a specific programme within our Marketing Plan.

A number of issues have to be successfully addressed when establishing a partnering arrangement:

1. early contact with the potential partner is important so that the process can evolve, or emerge from a strong mutual understanding of each organisations' strategic objectives, short and long term aims and the opportunities perceived;
2. for the department, or client-side, it is still important to get the specification right;
3. the form of the partnering arrangement, its legal footing, financial basis or profit sharing need to be encoded in the contract;
4. in the bid evaluation stage the strength of the partnering arrangement, its durability or flexibility, need to be considered;
5. there is still a need to demonstrate VFM;
6. the partnering arrangement opens up new contractual relationships and responsibilities; departmental staff as either partners of SLA/contract managers may need training in contract management;

7. on a practical level, working with partners is more time consuming, and it becomes more difficult to manage the pace of change & developments;

8. staff management issues need to be addressed; full measure Market testing is about competition and its language is couched in terms of winners and losers. Partnering arrangements may entail some loss of the two competitive weapons of confidentiality and freedom. Partners may be seen as cuckoos in the nest who in future years may be in a better position to bid for our work.

Maurice Line has recently asked "where does this pursuit of competitive advantage lead to?"[7] He is concerned about the real pressures put on libraries which may endanger the quality of services. To this extent, the challenge ahead for us is to combine the benefits of partnering arrangements with the overall purpose of marketing planning: the identification and creation of sustainable competitive advantage, and at the same time maintaining quality of services.

References

1. McDonald, Malcolm H B and Morris P: *The Marketing Plan: a pictorial guide for managers.* Butterworth-Heinemann, 1987.
2. Coote, Helen: *How to market your library service effectively (and enjoy it in the process!).* Aslib, 1994. (The Aslib Know How Series).
3. Rowley, Jennifer. "*Marketing information systems*". *Aslib Proceedings 46* no 77/8, July/August 1994, pp 185–187.
4. Webber, Sheila: "*Marketing library and information services*": *Inform*, July/August 1994. (Covers marketing jargon and a review of marketing literature with reference to libraries.)
5. *Competing for quality: buying better public services.* CM 1730. HMSO, 1991.
6. "*Partnerships in business grow*" *Financial Times* 28 June 1994.
7. Line, Maurice B: "*The pursuit of competitive advantage in libraries leads . . . where?*" *New Library World, 95,* no 116, 1994, pp 4 6.

A Survival Guide to the New World

Susan Hill
Instant Library Recruitment

To survive we must change: that is the challenge. When I started to think about this paper, I was not sure how much to let the conference title "Who Needs Libraries—Challenges for the 90s", limit my imagination. If I emulate my two grandmothers and live to 94 with sound mind and body what will there be to see of libraries in the year 2044? This is frightening, 2044 is almost halfway through the 21st century, and I cannot begin to visualise it. One grandmother was born in 1870 and lived until 1964. Think what changes she would have seen, say, in communications. When she was young there were no cars, no telephones. She went by sailing ship to New Zealand. How many weeks would that have taken? A letter home to the family would have been as many weeks there as back: months in between correspondence. Now if I want to talk to my mother I just pick up the phone and call her. If I need to send her something in writing it can go by fax. I can E-mail my brother-in-law. Talk to my sister on our videophone. And I can get there in 24 hours. Incidentally my grandmother never saw television as it came to our area the year she died. Could she have visualised it in 1914 when she was 44?

The title for our conference could easily have been "Changes in the 90s". Change is about challenge; change is a challenge. Change creates challenges and that is really what we are considering. Sadly change—the unknown— also creates fear and stress. Change can become a threat. If you allow change to threaten you then you will not survive: take steps now and equip yourself. Take a lead from the Boy Scouts and Be Prepared.

Since I first talked about this subject at the Institute of Information Scientists (IIS) Conference in 1987, a lot has changed. Many libraries and information centres did not have computers in 1987, and certainly many library and information people were computer illiterate. In fact, for every person interviewed wanting a job with daily use of computers, there was one who was adamant they did not want to use them at all!

Sir John Harvey Jones in *Managing to Survive*[1] said "Without question, the most desirable management skill for the nineties will be the ability to manage change. This is one of the rarest and most difficult skills to learn." Managing turbulent change is a key issue for senior people working in or without organisations today. In the past large scale change appeared to be an exception. Every so often there was the need to update systems, structure or perhaps technology and then the organisation returned to its "normal" stable state. As the pace of change accelerates the seemingly placid spaces between the turbulence of change have become shorter and shorter. Today it is unrealistic to imagine that any organisation will maintain any stable state.

When it was an occasional problem, change seemed much simpler, it was not undertaken until a clear need was seen, and what needed to be done appeared obvious. Today as wave upon wave of change crashed through nations and organisations it no longer looks so simple. It is far less clear what changes will happen and when. Avoiding change until it is inevitable may mean we have left it too late. I believe that managing or dealing with change is something everyone in every level of every job or walk of life must take on board. Sir John Harvey Jones says that if you are doing things in the same way as you were two years ago then you are doing them wrong. No longer does "if it ain't broke don't fix it" apply. We should look for change. Management or staff, how we view these changes and challenges very much affects the way in which we deal with them. We need to learn to live effectively with continual change—to constantly reassess ourselves, our skills and our jobs. Quite simply, fear them, find them threatening or fail to cope with them and we (individuals, teams or departments) might sink, without trace.

Liz MacLachlan and Andrew Lapworth discuss government libraries before, during and after marketing testing. This is quite a dramatic change encouraged by a visionary government. Doubtless that government itself will change, perhaps in the 90s. Where will that leave you? The challenge will not go away, as any new government is also likely to be a government with vision. Perhaps it will be different. Who knows? One thing you can be sure of, the clock will not be turned back. Contracting out of services, outsourcing, contract management, 2–5 year contracts are here to stay in whatever form they present themselves.

We are going to hear about open government this afternoon from a Campaigner for Freedom of Information. It may take time and it may not progress to that stage until after the 90s here, but it will happen. More change. More challenge.

Two issues that will increasingly affect your working life are contracted out services and the exponentially rapid growth and expansion of IT. When I spoke at the IIS Annual Conference 1987 I identified several potential future changes. Most of those have now overtaken us but two that are still affecting us all today are an increase in the use of technology, and a slow but identifiable expansion of information skills into a wider environment. I would edit those now to say a *rapid* increase in the use of technology, and I would also add a third point— changes in working practices.

Throughout I have emphasised that a good and successful information provider needs to be a delicately balanced combination of communicator, salesperson, negotiator, diplomat, technologist, to have an endless supply of information, initiative and knowledge, coupled with business, management and administration skills. Good people are the most valuable asset you have. Ongoing education and training are very real necessities. Ignoring this is false economy.

That brings me neatly to *you*, the reader. You are the people who are going to have to survive in the new world, to face the challenges of the nineties. You are going to have to take responsibility for yourselves. Speaking as a recruitment consultant, I see many different approaches from people. I see different attitudes, different ways of dealing with things, differing views. I see people who succeed, people who fail. People with clear ideas of their future, people with completely open minds and those who are simply unable to think for themselves. Just asking an interview candidate why they are looking for a new job can open a floodgate of potentially damaging information. I see, and am always impressed by, people who strive to continue their own development, sometimes against the most appalling odds. I despair of those who sit waiting for something to happen, particularly when I know it is within their means to make that effort. Usually blaming the ubiquitous "they". In what is left of the 90's, caring though they have been dubbed, there will be no room for those who fail to attend to their own development.

The educators are now continually rethinking their strategies. Witness just the 18 or so British institutions recognised as providing an education in librarianship. Since the 80s, all have changed their degree titles to include the word information. Most offer a choice of Information degrees. Nearly all offer more than one path of study. Course content now changes virtually every year. New, innovative and interesting joint courses are being developed.

Educators are aware that going to school, then university and perhaps university again is no longer enough. They see that there are those who need to continue to develop, who did not get a chance first time around, who chose the wrong course first time or those who wish to continue to extend their studies. There are many options. Distance learning courses have been up and running for some time, giving the chance to those who wish to do a Masters in Librarianship, or perhaps something with a Management element in it. Possibly a Diploma in Management Studies or even an MBA. There are courses that enable you to study in your spare time (evenings and weekends) that allow for units of study already completed in other institutions. There are courses that enable you to pick and mix. Modular Access programmes that aim to provide intellectually challenging courses, cater for your particular needs and interest, with enough flexibility for you to study full or part-time, in the day or the evening over one year or two. The government and other institutions offer interest free career development loans aimed at those who wish to progress. If you want to further your education, there is really nothing now to stop you, unless you simply cannot be bothered to make the time or the effort.

In London and other centres, although the costs have increased, there are still opportunities to study the most amazing range and variety of subjects via adult education institutes. Many companies and professional bodies involved in the Information world offer short (half to three days) practical courses, where librarians can learn about records management, management skills, the Internet. Make sure that you, your manager or your department is on those mailing lists.

This brings us to Professional Development and Professional Involvement. Sometimes our natural British sangfroid inhibits us from developing or becoming involved. There are those who hold back, not sure of what they could offer, or learn, from involvement in organisations such as the LA, IIS, ASLIB, as well as the Circle of State

Librarians. Some pay their membership and pay little heed to what goes on. There are those who pay and then sit back and criticise what the again ubiquitous *they* do. These organisations are not *they*, they are *you*. You have to get involved to help them function, prosper and have something to offer. And not just yourself, encourage others to get involved.

You can gain much in return:

- Contacts—networking;

- experience and skills from Committee work and contribution;

- knowledge—from attending talks, seminars, workshops and conferences;

- presentation skills—contributing to talks, seminars, workshops and conferences;

- keeping up to date reading the specialist and related literature.

Sharing knowledge and experience is as important as learning.

If there is no money in your budget to attend the next IIS conference, and you cannot afford to pay out of your own pocket, why not offer your services to the organising committee. Volunteers are always welcome, and you can probably then have a free place, or at least listen to those parts that are of particular interest. Not only does such committee work and involvement look good on your cv, it teaches you practical new skills.

At this point I must mention NVQs. NVQs—SVQs in Scotland— are being developed within our profession by the Information and Library Services Lead Body (ILS–LB).[2] It is thought that by 1996, 40% of the workforce will have NVQs. An NVQ is a competence based qualification, which shows a person can carry out a certain task in a competent manner. Employees who gain an NVQ have demonstrated that they have the range of skills at nationally agreed standards to carry out their job. The crucial difference with academic qualifications is that NVQs are gained by practical assessment on the job.

One benefit that I see with NVQs is that credits can be gained from other disciplines such as financial management and human resources thus allowing competency in non-core library skills to be recognised.

David Whitaker, the first chair of the ILS-Lead Body has said "We must treat this as an opportunity to professionalise information and library services at all levels by the 21st century. It is in the interests of those working in the sector for the sake of their own survival, and more importantly, for those whom they provide services and the country at large."

The message I want to bring you about Education, Training, Continuing Professional Development and NVQs is simply that if you have not done so already, from today you must take the responsibility for these important areas into your own hands. The educators *must* provide us with open access education—but *we* must access it.

I have asked many people what they see as the Librarian/ Cybrarian/Information Manager skills for the future. It was interesting that nobody really mentioned IT skills. The computer in the home and workplace has nearly progressed to the stage that the ballpoint pen did when it brought scribble power to us all: it is accepted and used by all. It is no good thinking that learning about computers will help you survive. You should know about them already and be completely comfortable with their use in a variety of situations. You have no option now but to invest your own time and money in developing these skills if they are not up to an acceptable level. It is particularly important to know *what* can be done with computers and software. Having keyboard skills doesn't mean you will be used as a secretary, nor does admitting to computer literacy mean you will be labelled a potential programmer. Far from it.

So what skills are you going to need? I listed above what a good and successful information provider needs to be. Without doubt you need a little of each of these skills to be a good all rounder. What you need to be able to do is to recognise your strengths, and identify how you can capitalise on them. Another option is to develop some of them so that you become a specialist—and hence invaluable—in a specific area. It is interesting to look at a study done by a group of students in 1990. Over 140 jobs that were advertised in the *LA Record* Vacancy Supplement were followed up with questionnaries asking, among other things, "What skills would be considered essential when selecting candidates both to interview and at interview". Overall the skills wre ranked thus:

- Management;
- Information;
- IT/computer literacy;
- library and information;
- communication;

43

- business;

- general.

The change in emphasis of skills required is particularly obvious to me in both my role as a recruitment consultant, and as an information professional monitoring the current library and information science literature. Clients in *all* sectors ask for a wide range of additional skills. Often not even mentioning the library and information skills, not because they are not wanted, but because they are taken as read.

Let us just look at some of the skills that you will need. The list is not exhaustive, and you don't need them all. Establish which ones you have and wish to develop. Understand your strengths so that you can promote and use them when the time comes. It is a constant source of amazement to me how humble people are, how they stammer and stutter about their skills and abilities. Often describing the mundane aspects of their jobs, and little about the "good" bits, the interesting tasks and the dynamic skills.

Let us break down these skills, summarise their span:

Management Skills
    Personnel or man
      management;
    finance;
    budget;
    information;
    project;
    team leading;
    market planning.
Information Skills
    Management;
    interpretation;
    analysis;
    added value;
    retrieval & research;
    storage;
    organisation;
    dissemination;
    presentation;
    quality.

IT Skills
    Wordprocessing;
    databases;
    spreadsheets (and
      statistics);
    on-line databases;
    CD-Roms;
    automated library systems;
    Internet;
    E-mail;
    graphics;
    undertaking of what can be
      done with IT and software.
Library and Information Skills
    Cataloguing;
    classification;
    abstracting;
    indexing;
    automation;
    retrieval;
    thesaurus construction.

Communication Skills
 (always remember this is a
 service industry)
  interpersonal;
  presentation;
  writing;
  personality;
  character fit;
  PR & marketing;
  languages.
Business Skills
  planning;
  financial;
  problem solving;
  corporate understanding;
  PR & marketing;
  consultancy;
  strategic planning.

General
 flexibility;
 adaptability;
 ability to work under
  pressure;
 ability to work to deadlines;
 enthusiasm;
 logic;
 understanding of the work
  environment;
 proactivity;
 team working.

Marydee Odjala in "Core Competencies for Special Library Managers of the Future" says ". . . you do not climb the ladder of success, but navigate the spider webs of information, constantly learning as you go. In an information-intensive future, the role of Cybrarian is critical. Not only can this person identify, provide, analyse, organise, categorise, and disseminate information, this person can create information".[3]

Her core competencies will probably be stage two of the development of NVQs. They are aimed at a time in the 21st century: 2005. With the rapid state of development, there is a good chance that much of what she envisages will be on us in the 90s. The information superhighway we hear so much about, is really a maze. As information managers move in and control and guide its development, it will become even more accessible to others. In fact it will not be long before what we see of it now is just an old dirt track in terms of sophistication. The skill that I see as the most important for the survival of anyone in the future is simply flexibililty.

Flexibility is the most important skill, the key to the future. But, of course, it is not just in our field that things are changing. Changes are occurring across the board. New ways of operating are appearing in all functions of life. We must respond to these historical changes, or we will become an anachronism. The future is about Change.

Again, we need to take the widest view. Other influences will be:

- continued growth in the amount of and the demand for information;

- the economic value and the intellectual content;
- global movement of information;
- partnerships with information users;
- decreased availability of financial and human resources;
- and change in work practices.

The recession has in many ways crystallised our thinking about work, jobs, and job tenure. The growth in employment agencies, especially in our field of library and information work, has been a good thing. When I started in the field in 1987 temping and short contracts were viewed with suspicion by many. When applying for jobs and attending interviews questions were invariably asked about lack of continuity, eyebrows were raised if you had been made redundant or lost your job. It signified failure. Now everyone sees that it is the job or post that is made redundant and that the individual is just occupying that role at the time. So many people in the private sector have had their jobs made redundant, some even two or three times, that it is a rare employer now who looks askance at such a blip in work history. For temporary work can be a tremendous way of gaining new skills, experiencing different types of work and different work environments. It is an acknowledged fact that there is now no such thing as a job for life, job security. That may seem difficult to some of you in the Civil Service, especially if you have had your head down ignoring what has been going on outside. Its no longer true that you stay till you die at your desk.

If your department is one of those that at some stage will inevitably be run by private contractors or external management, do you think they will want you? Thinking is emerging that takes into account the fact that our working life is no longer forcing our way up a career ladder. We must accept that nothing stays the same for ever in our lives. Your career life can be split into three major parts. First, the 20s—when your education and early work practice prepares a base of skills and knowledge. Then the 30s and perhaps the 40s where you probably work the hardest and achieve the most. Strengthening that base and developing it. Finally into the third work age (not to be confused with the University of the Third Age aimed at those 60 plus) when deliberately or inadvertantly you become independent. No one is screaming for you, so you do the things you want to do. With luck you will be financially secure and your responsibilities have lessened. The rump of the mortgage is paid and the kids have flown the nest. Between these three stages there is new learning to be undergone. Part of the continual learning process.

How will you ensure that someone will want you? Are you adaptable? I don't emphasise how highly I regard adaptability as a skill. New work practices will undoubtedly mean that you will find that you change your job more readily and regularly than in the past. It is unlikely that you will always remain in the Civil Service. That reminds me to implore you to think about your future. Not just your self development but also life after work. It is never too early to start planning your pension. Something that you do not even have to think about safe in the arms of the Civil Service.

One of the things that I have come up against when recruiting is the narrow mindedness of organisations and their refusal to accept that people can change and adapt. "We must have someone who has worked in an academic environment before". "We don't want anyone from outside the banking world, they will not understand us." "Public librarians cannot transfer to the private sector" and vice versa. It is easy to accept those generalisations and fail to argue that generalisations do not take individual human adaptability and endeavour into account. I think that new working practices will slowly alter this stereotyped and stilted thinking. The information skills must be king, and the environment in which they are applied surely secondary. You as information professionals must not become marginalised as others see the enormous intellectual and economic value of managing information and take over from us. As the information world expands rapidly so must you expand to survive. You must continually add to and expand your skills portfolio, and work with other disciplines. You must strive to understand the potential of information management within organisations, rise within those organisations and develop that management of information to a pivotal role.

The information environment is influenced by demographics, economic conditions and technology. Telecommunications will soon give one person access to another without the need to know where he/she is. (Only yesterday I read an announcement that the Japanese have developed a wristwatch telephone.) No longer will the phone or communication transponder be fixed to the wall in the hall, you will carry it and your own personal access number around with you. You will probably even carry your work around, allowing you to be where you are most needed, able to work and be accessed. At home, with a client.

As I said at the beginning, when my granny left Ireland in the late 1800s she could hardly have foreseen the way that trains, planes and automobiles would revolutionise our lives. Now it is the turn of communications technology to revolutionise the ways in which we live and work. When I am 94 I may be able to deliver this talk, glance at my watch and realise that I have only nano seconds to get to my next appointment. No problem: I will simply raise my eyes heavenward and say "Choyi Chiuu". For those of you who do not speak Klingon— "Beam me up Scotty".

References

1. Jones, Sir John Harvey: *Managing to Survive.*
2. "Scottish/National Vocational Qualifications. *Inform* No 166 July/ August 1994.
3. Odjala, Marydee: 'Core Competencies for the Special Libraries of the Future". *Special Libraries 84* No 4 Fall 1993.

Open government: fact or fiction

Maurice Frankel
Director
Campaign for Freedom of Information

Let me give you a few examples first of all of the climate that we are dealing with. I will read you some quotes, and you can see if you can guess who is speaking, before I tell you.

"I have to say I have not the slightest intention of giving you any information why I reached the decision I did. To sum up, I will please ask you in future if you will please direct your enquiry to me personally. But I can assure you, you will certainly not receive any answers."

That was the Chief Constable of Merseyside in a letter, not to me, or to an ordinary member of the public, but to the Chairman of the Police Complaints Authority. When I read this I thought something has gone terribly wrong and I phoned up the Police Complaints Authority and they said: "We don't even have to check. We remember that very well."

Another explanation, why information will not be disclosed:

"Because it is a matter of principle, there is no requirement for us to provide this information to other people. We do not have to justify ourselves to any one or any organisation other than the Department of Transport"—the supreme moral authority of the land—"This is all we are required to do and this is all we are going to do." That was the Director of Engineering in Newcastle explaining why he will not release the cost-benefit analysis to justify a new road in that area which was being hotly contested by a number of people whose homes were going to be affected by it—because it was a matter of principle.

Now a topical example. A few months ago the news that Canada geese in Hyde Park were being culled leaked out against great security measures to keep this information quiet. And when the Royal Parks were asked what method was being used to cull the geese they refused to say, other than it was the most humane available. When he was challenged as to why he would not say, he said: "It is not a secret, we just decided not to say."

Finally my favourite of all:

"You cannot, of course, have detailed reports made available to every outside organisation and everybody who wants to come along and look at them. No, I will not show you the report, I see no reason to show the BBC the report. You know the content of the report"—because the speaker has just given what is her version of it—"If you don't believe me that is tough luck."

This was broadcast on a Radio 4 programme by Anne Widdicombe when she was Minister of Social Security. I am particularly fond of this one because I think it reveals an underlying truth about the British Constitution. It is what I call the tough luck principle: "We have the information. You do not, and if you do not like it—tough luck."

When I speak to other audiences, normally they say, well this is the kind of thing that affects the general public, but of course it doesn't affect MPS or Parliament. But of course it does affect MPS and Parliament. They have no greater right to information, individual MPS, than the ordinary citizen. The only advantage they have is they have the right to ask questions in a well publicised forum in Parliament and so it is potentially more embarrassing, only potentially more embarrassing, if they are refused without good reason.

I will just give you two or three examples. I'm sure you all know these. Some of you have probably constructed these replies yourselves, so it will come as no great shock to you to hear this. Firstly, Mr Beith to ask the Chancellor of the Exchequer "If he will list debts of over £100 million owed to the government by private sector companies not including debts from last year's yet unpaid tax bills." The Minister replied "The information requested is not held centrally and could be obtained only at disproportionate cost". I think this tells you two things. First of all, most interesting, I think it tells you why we are in such financial trouble. Because the government thinks it is too expensive to figure out who owes it more than £100 million. But I think it also shows the casualness, almost the contempt with which MPS' questions are set aside.

Another question: "To ask the Secretary of State for Northern Ireland what arrangements there are for consulting consumers on the work and decisions of his department." Now anyone here who has worked in government for more than six months could probably draft the answer to this PQ without knowing anything about Northern Ireland. The Minister replied: "The information requested is not held centrally and could be provided only at disproportionate cost." That is farcical, really, because you know you could actually draft the real answer to that question in 15 minutes.

Here is another; to ask the Home Secretary "Whether he will publish in any form that does not jeopardise national security the approximate total number of files accessible by the name of the individual held by the security services". Not who the files are held on, just the number of files. "It is not possible to disclose such details without jeopardising the service's operational capability". Now, I have thought hard about the mechanism by which the security service's operational capability will be harmed by revealing that it is 50,000, 5 million, or 50 million. Whatever the figure is, how would it jeopardise the security service's operational capability? Someone says "Ah! there's only 5,000. That means they haven't got one on me."

Now, what is going on here is a culture of secrecy in which it is accepted that too much information exposes the Minister to difficult questions. Partly I think the answer is that Ministers are not on top of their briefs, and they know they could not handle any questions other than the one that has been anticipated, and therefore the less information they give out the less likely they are to be challenged to answer further questions to which they do not know the answers. But it also acts to protect the government from criticism; to prevent people who want the government to do something else, from being able to document, to substantiate, the case they want to put to the government. It allows the government, if it has decided it is not going to do something, to keep it off the agenda. Simply by refusing to answer questions which might document the case for doing that precise thing. And this is one of the reasons why across the world in any society one of the great areas of contention over secrecy is nuclear power. And one of the reasons that it is, is that there is so much investment in nuclear power, it is so expensive to do, that the government is so unwilling to be challenged on it. And therefore it is, whether in the United States, in Europe, in Scandinavia, always an area of high secrecy.

I think one of the best accounts was provided by William Waldegrave. He was attacked for it, in one sense I think unjustly, because I think it's an insight into government thinking. He said:

"In a free society, most government is a matter of negotiation. Totalitarian governments do not have to negotiate. They just tell you. Negotiations take place not only with other governments but constantly at home with warring and contradictory pressure groups, financial markets and Parliament"—these are the warring partners with whom this government is constantly at war—"Administration is much more like playing poker than playing chess. One cannot always have all the cards face up."

Now that, I think, is an interesting insight into how government thinks but it is also inaccurate in an important way. Because all the partners in a chess game or a poker game have an equal chance of winning, depending only on chance, literally, or their skill. One's dealings with the government are influenced by other matters, in particular the monopoly that the government has over information and its actual willingness to turn the cards up only at its own convenience.

Here are two different accounts of how Ministers and the government deal with Parliament. The Prime Minister was asked "What is the government's basis for answering parliamentary questions?" He said that, except for confidential matters or when successive governments have refused to answer, or where it is too expensive "Answers should give the information sought, and should be accurate and truthful and not misleading".

Now that is one version, of communicating with Parliament. Here is the alternative from no less an authority than Lord Tebitt. "I do not think there is any doubt in my mind that anybody who holds ministerial office has given a reply which leaves the questioner to come to a wrong conclusion. Parliament must not be told a direct untruth, but it is quite possible to allow them to mislead themselves." That gives us a more profound insight into the nature of government relations with Parliament than the Prime Minister's answer.

Now one of the great events in the freedom of information calendar, I think a lifetime event is going to be the Scott Enquiry which is to be published in 1995. For anyone going along to that, one of the most remarkable things is seeing the clash of cultures between Lord Justice Scott, who is used to people answering questions in court where you are not allowed to withhold information for reasons of convenience or embarrassment and the Whitehall witnesses for whom convenience or embarrassment are central to whether information is disclosed. The pinnacle of those exchanges was when the Cabinet Secretary appeared, and he was asked to explain the government's policy towards providing information to Parliament. Of course the whole basis of the events which led to the Scott Enquiry were failures to disclose a change of policy to Parliament. At first an official admitted it was a change of policy, and then the government quickly corrected themselves. They said "The official who said that had misinformed himself. The policy had not changed." The official line was that the policy had not changed. The person who accepted that it had changed had misinformed himself.

So Sir Robin was asked questions about this relationship and he gave the Prime Minister's answer, that answers are full and accurate and truthful and not misleading. And he then, on his own initiative, chose an example to illustrate that. And the answer he chose, to the amazement of everybody present including Lord Justice Scott, was the government's answers to questions about contacts with the IRA. If you remember, the government said "We are not talking to the IRA, we are not negotiating with the IRA" and the Prime Minister said "It would turn my stomach"—that was the evocative phrase he used—"to talk to Gerry Adams or the IRA." No sooner does he announce this, than the IRA publishes all the detailed correspondence. Sir Patrick Mayhew says "Well, we have not actually talked to them." The IRA then revealed that there had been two face to face meetings between unnamed officials and the IRA, government officials who are generally supposed to have been members of the security services. To which the government's response was "These were unauthorised". Whatever happens nothing changes the validity of the government's argument. So now the amazing thing is that while he did not go into these details, Sir Robin cited in general terms the answers about dealings with the IRA as examples to demonstrate that the government does not mislead Parliament. This is what he said:

"It was a half answer, if you like, but it was an accurate answer"—no talks or negotiations—"and went to the point of what people were concerned about. . . . This was an answer which was true but not complete, not designed to mislead. . . . Half a picture can be true. . . . My justification of that answer is, I think, not because it was justified in the circumstances, though I think it was, but in that situation it did not mislead. It gave half the picture."

Now this is a stunning answer because the one thing you can say on the government's behalf is that these negotiations and discussions with the IRA were so important, so central to the process of saving lives that it was necessary to do them even if you could not admit it. I suspect most people would have accepted that it was valid for the government to talk to the IRA, and to accept that the public were going to be misled in the circumstances. And if Sir Robin had said, "Well the public were misled. We regret it, but we think the people understand the need for it." That's one thing but note he does not say that, he does not justify it on the grounds of necessary deception. In other words this answer conformed to the normal, high standards of Whitehall truthfulness. And this is what I think is most disturbing. This is not an exception to the policy of truthfulness, this is truthfulness at its pinnacle according to the Whitehall view. And that is why people outside Whitehall think that something absolutely fundamental has to be done to the way in which we learn about what the government is up to. Because the whole basis of the training of officials for briefing Ministers to answer questions is, in Norman Tebbitt's words "To allow MPs to mislead themselves".

This is not a party political point, as anybody who is old enough to remember a previous government will remember. Similar kinds of things happened then too. For example, the whole of the Chevaline project, which was the replacement for Polaris, was agreed by a Labour government without even informing the Cabinet. Three Ministers decided on it. When the Conservatives came in they revealed that this policy, introduced in secret to upgrade Polaris, had been done at a price of £1,000 million. Sometime after Francis Pym, who was the Conservative Defence Secretary, has announced this an unidentified Labour Minister involved in the original decision told the newspaper anonymously that this was "One of the most outrageous, disgusting, most damaging examples of breaking the continuity of nuclear decision making there has ever been". To reveal what had gone on in the decision to replace Polaris and the cost of it.

Now I am just going to digress for a little while before we come back to the central theme, and talk about how secrecy directly affects the individual. The Campaign, particularly in the years when it was clear that a Freedom of Information Act would not get anywhere, in Mrs Thatcher's time, has been introducing smaller, private member's bills on individual subjects, four of which have become law. Many of these are on access to personal files of one kind or another. In other words giving people the right to see their own records. Housing and Social Work reports, or reports a doctor writes to an insurance company or employer about you, another bill opened up certain kinds of environmental safety information, and another, manually held medical records from November 1991. Anything written since November 1991 is now accessible to you by right. In the course of this we accumulated examples of what was going on in these files, unknown to the subjects.

The following were from school reports to the juvenile court. When a youngster is convicted of an offence at the juvenile court the school is asked to send in a report before sentencing. An academic who was also a JP did a research project looking at what was on these reports and found comments such as the following:

"Devious, plausible, manipulative and shallow."

These were reports from a head teacher:

"A liar and a thief"

"Could not accept authority in the school football team"

"I believe he is moving inexorably towards a life of crime in terms of imprisonment" [a hint by the way if you read between the lines] "He affects a nice side to his character, but this is not genuine"

My favourite—"Jimmy is a cancer to the student body. If he did not commit this offence, then someone else in his family did".

Housing: "I knocked on the door and it was opened by a middle aged floozy."

Social work: "A person of fairly limited intelligence and a rather bovine personality."

Medical reports: "A doll-like woman"; "Totally self indulgent albeit within a very soft, sugary package"; "Her husband seems surprisingly sensible".

"I've seen the patient, I've seen his wife. I've seen his two kids and I've seen their pet rabbit. And in my opinion the rabbit is the most intelligent of the lot of them".

So one of the things we said was how are we going to stop this? We are going to stop this by allowing people to see what is written about them. These abuses have real consequences for people's lives, maybe not the absolutely hilarious one, but the more damning ones have direct consequences for people's lives. We have promoted these Bills. It is a little metaphor of what goes on because the professions and the government were absolutely opposed to all this legislation at first. They had to be fought for tooth and nail. And the one thing you will notice about all these personal files rights is that none of them affect central government. The government allowed it through. The Access to Personal Files Bill originally would have applied to government records as well, but government records were all stripped out. The government only allowed it through on this limited basis.

One of the early bits of Freedom of Information legislation is the Public Bodies Admission to Meetings Act, 1960, introduced by Mrs Thatcher in her first six months as a Member of Parliament when she came top of the private member's ballot in late 1959. And she introduced a bill to allow the press and public to attend by right Council meetings, which was not a legally established right at that time. And you can go to the PRO and you can see how the government, the Conservative Macmillan government dealt with Mrs Thatcher, which is identical to the way Mrs Thatcher's government dealt with us, absolutely identical. They said to her, they were massively embarrassed that she was doing this at all. They were even more embarrassed because they had a commitment in their own manifesto to do something about it which they did not intend to act upon. They basically said we will support you if you do an absolutely minimum bill, which we will draft. If you insist on drafting your own bill to do what you want to do we will kill it. Under great reluctance Mrs Thatcher finally did the deal, to do that. But she kept threatening to renege on the deal. And the officials kept saying how worried they are that Mrs Thatcher is not going to stick by the deal and introduce the hopeless bill the government has drafted for her. And finally she gets called in by Dame Evelyn Sharp, you may remember from the Crossman diaries, who was Permanent Secretary of the Ministry of Housing and Local Government. And Dame Evelyn laid down the law to Mrs Thatcher. This is what the PRO reveals: "At my talk with her, I thought it was quite clear. I said the bill would have to be one through which an ill-disposed local authority could drive a coach and horses."

We have had the tough luck principle, and then when they are forced to do something we have the coach and horses principle—the second guiding principle of British government.

So what are we to make of the Code of Practice on Open Government, in light of that. The first thing to say is that you are probably the only gathering of 150 people anywhere in the country that has heard about it. In fact we will be lucky if there *are* 150 other people who have heard about it. The reason for that is partly because this Code was brought into force on a bank holiday in the Easter recess. Its total publicity budget is £51,000. Bear in mind the cost of publicising and giving away copies of the Citizen's Charter and little Charterlets is somewhere in the region of £20 million. The cost of telling people they now have a right to information from the government I think is an interesting indication.

Let me say what I think the advances of the Code are. This is the Code which essentially applies to central government bodies within the jurisdiction of the Parliamentary Commissioner for Administration, the Parliamentary Ombudsman. And the most important part of the code is that the Government says that Departments will in future reveal information in response to specific requests unless it falls within one of the 15 broad categories of exemption in the Code itself. If people are unhappy with what they get, they can appeal within the department against the decision. If they are still unhappy they can appeal, via an MP, to the Parliamentary Ombudsman. So we have created for the first time a right of independent appeal against the government's refusal, which is very significant. The Ombudsman has the statutory powers under the legislation which established his Office, to examine any government papers other than Cabinet and Cabinet Committee papers, and to call witnesses. In fact anyone who refuses to hand over a file or obstructs him can be referred to court for essentially being in contempt of court. So he has great powers to find out what is going on so long as Cabinet is not involved. Once the Cabinet is involved he is blocked from getting at it.

The second thing is that although there are a fantastic range of exemptions and they are fabulously broadly defined—I give some examples below—there is a provision which says that information can be disclosed if the public interest in disclosure outweighs the possible harm of releasing it, which is potentially quite important.

There is a separate, even littler publicised provision, which says that departments will make available the internal rules and guidance which they use when dealing with the public. And that is potentially very important. This is something which comes originally from the American Freedom of Information Act which has been copied into most other countries freedom of information law and was in the Right to Know Bill which Mark Fisher promoted last year which we drafted and which the government had adopted as well and that is potentially very important.

Finally—this is a staggering comment on the history of British administration—there is for the first time a commitment to giving people reasons for decisions affecting them. It is very welcome, but it is astonishing that this is 1994 and this is a constitutional innovation.

On the other hand the Code has a number of defects. These are the main ones. The first is that the government says, and repeats time and time again in the White Paper, in the Code, in the Guidance on the

Code, there is no commitment to release documents. This is a commitment to releasing information not documents. What the government says is, people would normally get a letter explaining, summarising the information that they want. They will not be able to see the actual report or papers or correspondence from which the information comes. That is the single most important defect of the whole Code. Because all these civil servants, all your colleagues in all the offices on the other floors, have spent all their time perfecting their skills in giving Parliament this minimal amount of information, in allowing MPS to mislead themselves. Are these people suddenly going to come clean with the ordinary member of the public? No. Go back and ask them off the record if they are going to come clean and see what they say.

Secondly the exemptions are really very, very broad. I will just give you some examples of the letouts from the Code. "The Code does not require departments to provide material which the government does not consider to be reliable." You ask people in the Department of Employment whether they consider any increase in unemployment statistics month by month to be reliable. "It does not require the government to disclose information whose disclosure could be misleading." Well.

It includes an exemption for "Information whose disclosure might prejudice legal proceedings." Well nobody is surprised by that. "Or the proceedings of any tribunal, public enquiry,"—how does one prejudice a public enquiry?—"or other formal investigation, whether actual or likely, or whose disclosure is, has been, or is likely to be addressed in the context of such proceedings". No, there may be a public enquiry in two years into this matter. This information may be required as part of that public enquiry, therefore it is exempt under the Code of Practice. This is the kind of drafting that has gone on here.

There is the provision for fees to be charged. Essentially the government says that "Fees can be charged if requests would lead to additional work, and if the information is not of a kind that has previously been disclosed free of charge." We have potentially a great sanction against disclosure in the form of fees. Most departments now publish their fee charging policies and they vary considerably. Most of them allow some free official time, which at the better end is up to five hours of official time before they charge, though when they start charging it is usually at the rate of £15 to £20 per hour. At the worst end, and if there is anyone from the Home Office they may know which department I am talking about, we have one hour of free time before charges come in. One hour of time is just enough time to get the kettle on and figure out which filing cabinet the file is in before the £20 an hour or £15 an hour starts to add up. I think this is quite unacceptable.

Some departments have policies of a standard flat fee, regardless of how much time is spent, of £15 an hour. Both MAFF and the Foreign Office has this policy [Since giving this talk the Foreign Office has dropped its £15 minimum charge.] To be fair to them they have not actually charged me for any of the requests I have made to them. So they may be holding fees in reserve as a sanction against what they regard as difficult or voluminous requests. I think those are the worst because they are basically saying all requests are potentially chargeable.

The next problem is the limited jurisdiction of the Code. It only applies to bodies within the Parliamentary Ombudsman's jurisdiction and they are listed in the leaflet the Cabinet Office produced. It does not apply to nationalised industries, police, security services, Monopolies and Mergers Commission, National Curriculum Council and to quite literally several hundred non-departmental bodies which are accountable to central government. All these functions which have gone out to the Quango-type bodies are excluded from the scope of the Code.

You have to go to the Ombudsman via an MP which is a pain, and which will discourage some people. And finally it is not actually enforceable. Now we do not actually know at the end of the day how much of a problem that will be because the government says that invariably people do what the Ombudsman tells them to do and do not reject the Ombudsman's recommendation and therefore if the Ombudsman rules that something ought to be disclosed the chances are that that will be as effective as a court ordering disclosure. We will have to see whether that will be the case. I think the problem will be where it is highly embarrassing for Ministers. If the information tends to show a Minister did not tell the truth, how will the Ombudsman deal with that situation. When its a matter of national security what will the Ombudsman do. In many cases I think it is right that the Ombudsman will be effective in securing disclosure. I have one example of how departments respond to the Ombudsman—the Welsh Office. This is the Select Committee on the Ombudsman saying "The Permanent Secretary to the Welsh Office still found it difficult to accept that the actions of his Office constituted maladministration. He had not studied the definition of the word maladministration. "Pretty poor administration" was his preferred description" So he says, we're not guilty. It was pretty poor administration not maladministration what we got up to. So I think there is room for dispute over the interpretation of the terms of the Code of Practice whether departments will be willing to abide by it.

But the most important aspect, the most controversial in several quarters was this bar on disclosing documents. We have now had the Ombudsman's first decision, announced last November, which was into an application for the report of a public enquiry into the Birmingham Northern Relief Road. This was a proposal which had been floated in 1988 or 1986. There had been a public enquiry. The inspector produced his report, but before the Secretary of State announced his decision the plan was withdrawn in favour of an alternate new plan which has now been put forward for a toll, a fee-paying road. The people who are now concerned about the new plan want to know what the inspector reported at the end of the original public enquiry. The Department of Transport has consistently refused over many years to release this report to MPS or objectors, on various grounds, in fact on an incredible range of grounds. Two MPS put in a complaint to the Ombudsman, who last week ruled in their favour and last week ordered that the report be disclosed. The interesting thing was the Department of Transport who had objected on every ground they could think of. Firstly it would be misleading because the route is slightly different. Then they said it was not relevant, then they said it would prejudice the public enquiry, and then they said it would affect internal candour, damage internal candour to reveal this. I should have said the big exemption in the Code of Practice is the one for policy advice, internal discussion and deliberation, very very broadly framed. The Ombudsman rejected each one of these arguments and then the Department said "Ah, but it's a document and we don't have to release documents" The Ombudsman said "The information sought in this case is what the inspector said in his report. That is a valid request. If the Department could find a way of releasing all the information in the report, without releasing the report itself, that would fulfil their obligations." The judgement of Solomon "The practical difficulties in such an approach lead me to the common sense conclusion that in this case it would be simpler and more effective to release the report."

If this is the line he is going to take it is going to transform the Code into something very effective. If he is going to say "You don't have to release documents so long as you release verbatim all the information in the documents" then this Code will bite. But if the Code is going to be applied in the way the government intended the Code to be read, when they wrote in the loopholes then I think we are going to have something very serious. And we will have to wait and see.

Very briefly I should talk about the one new statutory right we have recently had. We have had the Environment Information Regulations which came into force at the end of 1992. And these supposedly give the people a general right of access to environmental information held by public authorities, central and local, subject to a series of even worsely drafted exemptions than the Code of Practice because they do not even bother with tests of harm. Information relating to matters affecting international relations is exempted under this. Not information harmful to international relations, but information relating to matters affecting international relations. Acid rain comes from other countries and goes from Britain to other countries, it's an international matter. It is dealt with by international negotiation. That is sufficient for it to be an exempt area from disclosure under the environmental information regulations.

We did a survey on this. We tried to get information out of Thorp Nuclear Plant. We discovered first of all the most interesting thing was all the government agencies that claimed they weren't subject to these regulations at all. First was BNFL. They said "We are just like a private company. We are not covered by these regulations." Actually BNFL is publicly owned, all its shares are held by the DTI except for one which is held by the Treasury Solicitor. The DTI appoints the Chairman, Chief Executive, and the Board. It is listed in the Cabinet Office's Public Bodies publication as a public body, totally under the control of Ministers. They are refusing to disclose information on the grounds that they are like a private company.

The Health and Safety Executive refused to disclose information about nuclear matters on the grounds that they have no public responsibilities for the environment in the nuclear field. Actually the regulations do not allow them to distinguish between the areas they work in. It says if they have any environmental responsibilities, then information they hold on any subject is subject to these regulations. The interesting thing is the Health and Safety Commission's annual report a few years ago actually said that HSE's regulatory role in certain areas "implies substantial concern with environmental issues, and include policy and enforcement responsibilities under various regulations controlling the risk from nuclear or other major hazard installations." So the Health and Safety Commission's annual report says they have environmental responsibility for the nuclear industry. But when we applied for information, miraculously their responsibilities had changed, and the Health and Safety Executive had no statutory or other formal responsibility relating to the environment irrespective of nuclear sites. So they have wriggled out of them.

Best of all there was a body obscure to anybody who is not from the Department of the Environment's nuclear or environmental divisions here called the Radioactive Waste Management Advisory Committee. We applied to this body for information. They refused. I phoned up the Chairman and I said "On what grounds do you refuse to comply with the regulations" He said "What grounds are there?" So I said "There are two. Either you do not have public responsibilities for the environment or you are not under the control of Ministers." He said "Both". So this body says it is not under the control of Ministers. Ministers appoint the members of this Committee. Ministers set its terms of reference. They fund it. They supply its secretariat and premises. The Department receives copies of all its papers. Officials attend parts of its meetings. Ministers must give their consent before it can publish its advice. Ministers can dismiss members at any time without even serving out their contracted period, without giving reasons. Ministers can wind the Committee up altogether without giving reasons or without referring it to Parliament. This is a body which the Committee itself considers is not under the control of Ministers. So the convolutions the government will go to in order to avoid disclosing information. It is not a matter of they have to be seen to be believed, you don't actually believe them when you do see them!

The Observer newspaper did an opinion poll just before last Christmas. They asked: "Do you agree with the following—
'Generally the present government tells the truth'." 14% agreed; 77% disagreed; only 9% did not know. So we are talking about a situation where the government's credibility is very, very seriously damaged. On the whole, not occasionally, but generally most people feel the government doesn't tell the truth. In fact this is not party political. Because only 14% thought the present government tells the truth, only 19% thought the Liberal Democrats politicians tell the truth, only 23% thought Labour politicians generally tell the truth. So this is a general disillusionment and cynicism with the process of government and politics. And one of the reasons we have this is because government doesn't tell the truth. And one of the things that government needs to do in order to put its own house in order and regain its credibility is not to say it will tell the truth but to demonstrate by in our view a more fundamental reform than the one we have now, a Freedom of Information Act which is enforceable. The public have a right to this information.

All systems go.

At EBSCO we believe you should have the freedom to choose the best subscription service *and* the best automated system for your needs. These are two independent decisions with major implications for your library. That's why our efficient electronic services are compatible with most major library and serials control systems. So, you can have superior subscription service *and* your system of choice, too. Call us today to learn more about our independence-orientated library automation services.

EBSCO
SUBSCRIPTION SERVICES

Scotts Sufferance Wharf • 1 Mill Street
St. Saviour's Dock • London, SE1 2DF
Tel: (0171) 357 7516 • Fax: (0171) 357 7507

Where library automation is a liberating experience.

Challenge of the Superhighway: information via Internet & SuperJanet

John Reid

SilverPlatter Information Ltd

I would like to start by distinguishing between the superhighway and the Internet. These two terms are often used interchangeably, but there is an important difference. The data or information highway/ superhighway strictly refers to the future infrastructure for delivery of *all* types of digital data—text, graphics, audio, video, etc. The Internet (or the *Net*) typically refers to the current worldwide system for computer communication, mainly using TCP/IP as a protocol and telephone system infrastructure. My focus is more on the Internet than the superhighway.

What is the Internet? We need some definitions and descriptions. The Internet is a network of computer networks, a super communications system linking computers. It is a technological platform linking tens of thousands of networks and tens of millions of computers. It offers a vast array of new information services and products. It is dynamic, changing very rapidly. Its growth is exponential. It is a worldwide computer co-operative: a symbol of global collaboration. It represents convergence of the three key technologies: hardware, software and networking.

What are the characteristics of the Internet? It is a decentralised, self-regulating, democratic operation that is collaborative and altruistic. Its content is very variable and heterogeneous; some is excellent, some is terrible. So too with its performance. A key characteristic of the Net is that it is open, non-proprietary, and hence readily accessible. In terms of its effect it tends to be an equaliser, an organisational flattener. It is in line with current management theory: "bottom-up" rather than "top-down". In summary, it is many things to many people.

To put it in context; What systems are analagous to the Internet? The super highway term of course we are all familiar with, and its parallel to the highway/road system. The fact that you have to connect makes on-off ramps, minor roads, trunk roads and motorways relevant: the connection problem is important. Another analogue is the telephone system, with its comparable communication aspects. This is a universal system, the world's largest switched distributed network. It is similar also because it involves two-way communication—unlike, for example, cable-TV which is largely a one-way system. The postal system is also a useful analogy, because it moves parcels and letters very much as the Net moves information packets. So in a sense it is a better analogue than the telephone system.

What is the history of the Internet? I see this falling into three phases. The first—the military—covered the birth and early development of the Net. Its original concept in the mid-1960s had three characteristics still present today:

- no central authority;
- small packet data transfer;
- via multiple duplicate alternate routes.

The objective was to develop a system that would be reliable in the event of nuclear war. Interestingly, as early as 1968 the UK's National Physical Laboratory built a test network to evaluate this concept. The first actual implementation in 1969 was the start of what became ARPANET (from the United States Department of Defense's Advanced Research Project Agency) initially just connecting four computers. During the 1970s this system really started to take off, used primarily for computer time-sharing. Then E-mail started and a lot of people heard about it, primarily in universities, and found it pretty useful. The decentralised structure and simple protocols facilitated computers joining, and the network grew throughout the 1970s.

In 1983 the military developed their own system (MILNET) and they split off. Their influence was replaced by the National Science Foundation (NSF) and other government agencies in 1984, marking the start of the second phase. Although ARPANET was not finally disbanded until the end of the 80's. In the 1990s we saw NSFNET move out of the USA and the start of commercialisation. From 1994 commercial services started to take off, marking what I see as the start of the third phase.

Now let us take a brief look at how big this animal is. Statistics are a bit variable, and a lot of big numbers are being bandied about. In May 1994 there were 48,000 registered networks plus an estimated 35,000 with inter-connectivity. Most people agree the Net is more than doubling each year. In 1993 network growth rates of 160% (USA) and 183% (non-USA) were reported. In October 1994, 83 countries had direct connection. In July 1994, 3.2 million hosts were connected in the Net's addressing system which was an 81% growth over the previous 12 months. Assuming 10 users per host (in some cases there may be hundreds), this implies some 30 million users. Traffic levels on the major backbones are growing at 100% to 200% per year. File transfer or FTP accounts for the largest traffic sector. We get a breakdown something like this: FTP 37%; Web/gopher 13%; Mail 18%. Looked at by country we get:

- United States 62%
- United Kingdom/Germany 5% (each)
- Canada/Australia 4% (each)
- Japan/France 2% (each)
- 14 countries 11%
- 50 countries 5%

So how do we use it; how do we get connected to the Net? Typically you need an Internet service provider and many of these are now available. The options are a hard-wired connection (direct via a network or as a terminal via another host computer) or a dial-up connection (via a modem to a host computer). The trade off is between permanence and reliability versus flexibility. For many this decision will be made by cost. Connection costs will depend on the range of services and the bandwidth provided.

What are the range of services and platforms available? The major Internet services are:

- e-mail (point to point communication);

- Telnet (remote computer access/use);
- file transfer (to or from);
- information access (browsing: gopher, Web/directories);
- information access (searching: Archie/Veronica/WAIS);
- news/discussion: USENET (10,000 discussion groups); mailing lists; bulletin boards (46,000); Internet Relay Chat IRC/talk.

In terms of platforms the Net is largely a client server system. That means typically two machines talking to each other: a server that is delivering the information and a client that is accessing it. These are some of the platforms used on the client interface side:

- UNIX (the original academic favourite, still strong)
- DOS (now likely to be eclipsed by Windows);
- MAC (a small dedicated group);
- Windows (where most of the action is now);
- OS/2 (multi-tasking and IBM support make this useful).

On the server side UNIX predominates.

Let us now look at the client side in more detail, particularly information access via Web and gopher. I should say a little more about what the Web is. The Web is a hypertext search system, which permits you to jump from document to document. It sounds quite simple but in fact is suprisingly sophisticated and useful. It connects different protocols. Gopher an hierarchical system, although it has also recently added hypertext capabilities. Although popular and useful for information delivery in the library environment, Gopher seems a clumsier and less flexible protocol than the Web. In comparison the Web is a powerful way to cover a topic area putting together collections of information and—literally—hopping around the Internet, making connections that will help people get as broad a coverage of a topic as possible.

Currently the more popular client interfaces, or browsers, are in the freeware area and include:

- Mosaic (Windows)
- Cello (Windows)
- Lynx (DOS).

There are also packages on the commercial side. What is happening is that the whole thing is starting to expolode as commercial organisations get involved. The freeware came from the university sector. The problem with freeware is that it is typically poorly supported, and these products are moving into the commercial environment. A good example is Mosaic which has been licensed to at least five different organisations (eg "Internet in a Box"). There is going to be an explosion of new products to handle client interfaces to the Web, gopher and related Net protocols. These currently include Chameleon and several Mac applications. At time of delivering this paper Netscope which in a few months dominated the browser market had yet to be released, vividly illustrating the dynamic and fast changing nature of the Internet scene.

Searching for Information on the Net is a key issue that faces us all. No global search tools or protocols currently exist. However there *is* a variety of server/protocol specific search tools currently available (largely freeware). These include:

- HYTELNET (hypertext access to telnet resources);
- ARCHIE (searches FTP files);
- VERONICA (searches gopher menus);
- JUGHEAD (indexes a particular set of gopher servers);
- WAIS (searches databases and is used in (VERONICA);
- FINGER/WHOIS (searches for people on the Net).

The problem of the Web really has yet to be solved. No effective tools currently exist for searching Web information resources, though much research is underway in this area. It will be increasingly important as server numbers grow. Then we need to be aware of some exciting future developments: ROBOTS and KNOWBOTS for assisting data access, and Intelligent agents are the subject of extensive research. It seems likely that we will see these in standard use before the end of the decade. Now widely used Web based search systems such as Lycos, Harvest Yahoo, etc were very much in their infancy at the time this paper was delivered.

So much for the Internet's capabilities, now what about its problems and constraints. For me the Net is both very exciting, and incredibly frustrating. These appear the main problems:

- traffic congestion and network instability;
- unstable/poorly documented and integrated software;

- massive volumes of variable quality data, irregularity updated and frequently duplicated;

- inadequate tools for information search and retrieval;

- inadequate security and authentication systems to protect confidentiality and copyright;

- need for effective pricing and payment systems to promote commerce on the Net.

How does all this impinge on us in Europe? Let us look briefly at inter-networking in Europe. Most countries have their national research networks—in the UK it is JANET—very much in parallel to what happened in the United States with the NSF. The public sector has played a greater role in developments over here. Although moves towards privatisation should yield more competition and efficiency as privatisation and scale economies set in. The technology and the markets are generally a little less advanced in Europe than in the US. Top down imposed standards in Europe such as OSI and x25 are proving much less successful than the US grass roots developed standards such as TCP/IP which is now replacing x25. It seems the new standard, ATM (asynchronous transfer mode), may lead to a common standard. Current backbone speeds are typically 2Mbps in Europe as compared to 45Mbps in the USA. There is a growing awareness of the importance of international conformance to share research worldwide.

In the UK the Joint Academic NETwork is the national research network under the Department of Education, with management now transferred to a private company, UKERNA. JANET connects 200 sites involved with academic and industrial research, meeting acceptable use standards. It was set up as x25, but is now moving rapidly to Internet's TCP/IP standard network protocol. Line speeds of up to 2Mbps are likely to be soon replaced by SUPERJANET project operating at 34Mbps.

This brings us to the SUPERJANET project. This five year undertaking was launched in 1992 and involves collaboration between the UK academic community and British Telecom. It is expected to form the basis of the UK's future information superhighway. As of September 1994 16 sites had been connected at very impressive speeds with bandwidths of 140Mbps and several soon to have 155Mbps. However, the average speed is likely to be more like 34Mbps. The system is soon to be extended to 50 or more sites, and further higher education sites will be added as funds permit. Local clustered sites will be served by several high performance Metro-politan Area Networks.

SUPERJANET currently operates with dual IP and ATM data net-works, but it is expected to go all ATM in 1995. The network is very much in test mode, and is currently being used very little for infor-mation services, although there are many new ideas in test and development. The higher bandwidth network is intended for multi-media use. This was successfully demonstrated in November 1993 when Edinburgh medical students witnessed, via SUPERJANET, an operation being performed in London.

As far as my firm, SilverPlatter, is concerned, we have a newly signed agreement for the establishment and testing of a new database delivery service via SUPERJANET. Partners will be SilverPlat-ter to provide the software and data content, Sun Microsystems to provide the hardware and University College London who will host and manage the service over BT'S SUPERJANET network. During the six month trial, online access will be offered to 30 to 40 mainly biblio-graphical databases such as Medline and Agricola from both optical and magnetic storage. Systems are expected to go commercial about August 1995. With that sort of bandwidth we should get pretty good performance.

One important example of developments under SUPERJANET is the British Library's electronic document delivery work. Trials are cur-rently in progress via JANET, with faxed documents. The British Library Documents Supply Centre is testing a new version of the Ariel workstation for document delivery over the Net, and they are enthusi-astic about its long term potential. The British Library will have a 10Mbps connection to SUPERJANET, facilitating further testing. How-ever, a single standard transmission protocol for document delivery has yet to emerge. Copyright issues remain the major barrier to development.

Now let us look at the future. What are the trends and driving forces? If we look back ten years we see a personal computer which cost in real terms ten times what it does now and delivered about one tenth the power. The main technologies that are defining the new future include:

- PC hardware technology;
- optical fibre, wireless and communication technology;
- software enhancement in compression, interfaces, data protocols, data organisation/access;
- data digitisation and integration.

And the driving forces are new and converging technologies and a rapidly expanding market place, with significant demand from the entertainment industry, research and education.

Let us make some predictions for the year 2000. Gigabit technologies will reach desktops in most of academia and major government and business offices. Computer telephone and TV technology will have merged to produce a range of powerful affordable "boxes" for receiving/processing/transmitting in the cost range £200–£1,000. A profusion of new software will contribute to the power and ease of use of these devices, and new universal standards will emerge to promote competition and progress. Available services and market demand will ensure that most connections will be high speed offering video phone/conferencing, interactive TV, and a host of free and commercial services including digital libraries and information services. In the United States all school and public libraries will be connected to the Net. Current growth rates suggest that 1 in 3 homes could also be connected. The United Kingdom should not be far behind. Around the year 2000 it will be a real superhighway.

What is the importance of all this for libraries? New electronic media, online, CD and now Internet allow librarians to better meet information needs and are replacing traditional hard copy services. Rising journal prices and library budget cuts, interacting in a non-virtuous circle, are acclerating the move to electronic data. "Just in time" supply of documents is replacing "Just in case" purchase of journals. Personnel budgets are shifting from traditional cataloguing activities to new tech tasks of systems design, development, support and training. The trend away from back-room "acquisition/cataloguing/preservation" towards more user orientated services of information "access/delivery" will continue. Demand for search intermediation is falling as users become more computer literate and search services improve. Librarians are becoming the facilitators rather than the intermediaries.

Still looking at the future, let us consider an hypothetical very large all-digital library. How feasible is it? If we take the Library of congress at about 10 million volumes, make some allowance for video: a pretty huge chunk of the total—we arrive at the following crude approximation of data measured in terrabytes:

Media Form	Archives	Annual addition
Books	25	1
Journals	12	1
News	1	0.1
Video	30	5

Online dbases	2	0.1
TOTAL	67	7.2

Now if all this data were digitised the storage cost today would be about £10 million. Furthermore the approximate storage equipment costs for various sizes of all-digital libraries would be as follows:

	V. Large (eg: LC)	Medium	Small
Av. No. of vols (million)	10	1	0.1
Storage reqmnts (TB)	70	7	1
Storage equipmnt costs (£ million)	10	1.2	0.2

Even if it were several times this cost, these are not inconceivable numbers. This one might have a digital Library of Congress for, maybe, £50m. However the data digitising costs would be orders of magnitude greater—maybe 100 times. Though these would be one off costs.

So, what are the challenges facing librarians? The electronic technology is here. You are committed to CD-ROM, the Internet, etc; it can only improve and expand. For Internet newcomers first utilise this new technology for your own professional development and then see how it can best help your clients. I think librarians need to develop their new roles as information systems researchers, designers, consultants, educators, and as collaborators throughout the publishing/distributing process. We rely very much on librarians at SilverPlatter, but image is a problem. Surely librarians need to change their professional title to "information scientist" or even "cyberian", and so recapture ground now in the hands of their IT counterparts. The challenge is *change*. The opportunites for professional development and growth are exciting, and the need for information scientists is significant and growing.

References
1. John Reid's Net address is: "johnr@silverplatter.com".

Printed in the United Kingdom for HMSO
Dd297937 10/95 C15 G559 10170